THE BLACKDOWN
MYSTERY

A tale of UFOs, crash retrievals, low lives and high adventure.............

JONATHAN DOWNES

(with a foreword by Tim Matthews and
illustrations - the grotesque ones anyway -
by Richard Freeman)

Edited by Graham Inglis
Designed by Mark North and Jon Downes for CFZ Communications
Using Microsoft Word 2000, Microsoft , Publisher 2000, Adobe Photoshop CS.

Photographs © 2002 CFZ except where noted

First published in Great Britain by CFZ Press

CFZ Press is a division of:

CFZ PRESS
15 Holne Court,
Exwick,
Exeter.
EX4 2NA

© CFZ MMVI

ISBN: 978-1-905723-00-3

To:

Richard and Graham
but for whom and all that shit..................

The author and Graham Inglis (L) promoting the first edition of this book at Dorchester in April 2000

Introduction

This book has had a long and chequered history. Originally, as recounted in the opening chapters, it was written at the behest of my then publisher, Gerry Connelly of Domra Publications in the spring of 1999. He originally wanted me to write an investigation into a monumentally dodgy UFO `crash` case from the mid 1970s. At that time I would have done anything for the money, because I had no visible means of support, and I had my divorce to pay for as well as the upkeep of the world's premier Fortean Zoological organisation.

However, within days of me starting work on the book, it became perfectly obvious that I was never going to finish it.

The entire case was complete and utter nonsense, and even if I hadn't been terminally sick of UFOlogy by that particular time of my life, I wouldn't have relished the task of writing a treatise about "alien anti-gravity devices" to satisfy my publishers when I knew full well that there were no such things as aliens, nor indeed anti-gravity devices.

However, I still needed the money, and I needed it badly.

Much to my surprise, Gerry accepted my suggestion for an alternative book, and encouraged me to write the farrago of nonsense which eventually became *The Blackdown Mystery*.

I delivered the manuscript to him in mid July 1999, and a few days later I banked the cheque and looked forward to the book's publication. In August I flew off to America where I appeared as one of the speakers at the International UFO Congress in Nevada. On my return I found that I no longer had a publisher.

Gerry and I went our separate ways after months of disagreements about how my books should be marketed.. This is not the time nor the place for me to go into the details of our estrangement, nor would I want to. Sufficient to say that we shall not be working together again, which is his loss rather than mine.

The rights to all three books I had sold him reverted to me, and the first edition of *The Blackdown Mystery* (dedicated to, and comb-bound by, my then fianceé Linda-Teresa Merwood) came out in April 2000.

For various reasons it had been printed in a ridiculously tiny typeface which made it almost impossible to read. Two years later I am happy to be able to reissue it in its entirety (a few bad jokes which had been expunged from the original edition at the behest of my then beloved and others have now been reintroduced), and in a readable typeface. The addition of Richard Freeman's illustrations and a few photographs of places of interest from the text, as well as Tim Matthew's foreword, (which disappointed me by being so kind and not demanding that Richard and I be immediately incarcerated in a re-education camp) can only, I believe enhance the second edition of a book which was described upon its first release as "scurrilous and disgusting".

Bob Girard from Arcturus Books in Florida wrote:

```
" Cheeky, that's what this  is - a cheeky investiga-
tion of a lead first inspired by "the ramblings of a
cross-dressing  drug  addict  and  his  elderly  schizo-
phrenic boyfriend." Intrepid  members  of the CFZ are
up  to  the  challenge,  and  manage  to  entangle  them-
selves  thoroughly  in  the  bizarre  trappings  of  this
case.  This  is  the  soft  underbelly  of  ufology,  rife
with unsavory characters, plenty of drugs and booze..."
```

That sums it up quite well, I think.

However, the one question that I am asked more than any other regarding this book is, is it a novel?

My answer is "define the word NOVEL". Pretty well everything that happens in this book happened in real life although not necessarily to the people that I said it did. I have changed a few names and dates, and places. If you travel to Bridgewater, for example, you will find the pubs I mention, but you won't find Clive, and BUFOCRAPMROG exist purely within the interstices of my imagination although all its members are horribly real.

Is the book true? It is as true as any other book written about UFOlogy

and more true than most. In a world where folk who shall remain name-less can get paid two hundred grand for a farrago of nonsense about `Zoltan of the 12th Density`, I think that it is a heartening sign that the 50,000 odd words of amusing bollocks that I have called *The Blackdown Mystery* can make it as far as a second edition.

It amuses me, reading back over it, as it is, for all its faults, a reasonably accurate portrayal of a crazy time in my life when the CFZ and I were fueled by alchohol and bad behaviour, and when, as hinted at by Tim in his foreword, I had an unhealthy interest in men wearing black hoods and smelling of Semtex.

My life might be much saner than it used to be but the world is getting crazier and crazier by the year and the murky waters of UFOlogy are no longer ones in which I enjoy cavorting. Sadly, I still receive emails from eager schoolkids asking how they can become UFOlogists. If this little book can do just something to put them off the idea then I have achieved something worthwhile.

Love and peace

Jonathan Downes
Exeter,
September 2002

EDITOR'S NOTE

This third edition is essentially the same as the 2002 edition but with a few more pictures put in and a few more spelling mistakes taken out. It is still nonsense. Enjoy!

FOREWORD

The first time I met Jon Downes and his merry band of mayhem merchants it looked like the circus had come to town. Actually, Downes, ever loud, foul-mouthed and obviously a total degenerate, was on board a ferry bound for the middle of the Channel with myself and 1,000 others. His party of cross-dressers, foot fetishists and perverts was not a pleasant sight.

He found out who I was and grabbed my hand. *"So you're the infamous Tim Matthews,"* he exclaimed. At that moment I knew my life had just taken a turn for the worse. Quite why anybody in the Fortean or Paranormal community would take en eccentric, disturbing and grossly overweight slob like Jon seriously was anyone's guess but then that's half his charm.

Then, of course, I reflected on my own colourful past and concluded that we probably had a lot in common. Jon likes Scott Walker and I like the funky sounds of Acid Jazz. We both have a liking for black mercedes and women in uniform.

I rest my case.

Tim Matthews
(aka Agent Hepple)

"He'd probably claim that it was all a cover-up of some kind aimed at preventing me revealing the truth about flying saucers, and that there was a crashed UFO and its occupants hidden in a secret bunker below Whitehall"......

Pic by Graham Hallowell

PROLOGUE

There were a number of reasons why the British Prime Minister, the Right Hon. Tony Blair was feeling more than slightly paranoid on the morning of the 24th April 1999. Although the level of racial violence in the United Kingdom was not as high as it had been a decade or so before when organisations like the National Front had achieved a disturbingly high level of popular support, in recent months there had been a rise in violent episodes, many of them linked with a confrontational Urban Terrorist group called Combat 18. Combat 18 formed into close-knit cells which operate independently and without a central leadership. This 'leaderless resistance' is based on the model of US Nazi groups such as `The Order`. Members of C18 are drawn from the violent street activists of groups like the BNP, `Blood & Honour`, the Ku Klux Klan, and fascist football hooligans such as the notorious `Chelsea Head-hunters`. Combat 18 is an openly Nazi organisation (the numbers 1 and 8 refer to the initials of Adolf Hitler). It believes in attacking and murdering blacks, Jews, lesbians and gays, and other minorities, and publishes hit lists containing the names, addresses and telephone numbers of those it views as 'enemies of the white race' in a number of publications.

A nail bomb, only a week before, had injured 39 people in Brixton, a south London neighbourhood with a large Afro-Caribbean population, and a similar explosion that very afternoon would injure seven people in Brick Lane, the east London heart of Britain's Bangladeshi community. Blair, always one to seize an opportunity, had urged Britons to turn the nail-bombing campaign against gays and ethnic minorities into a positive boost for his ideology of "New Labour":

"The only good that can come out of these nail bombs is that they spur all of us, whatever race, age, creed or sexuality, to work harder to build the one nation Britain that the decent majority want, and to bring our community closer together," the PM told Sikh community leaders in the north of England, although earlier, writing in the *Sunday Times*, Mr Blair had acknowledged that it has been a frightening and distressing time to be part of a minority in Britain.

Sir Herman Ouseley, the Chairman of the Commission for Racial Equality agreed with him, telling GMTV that *"There comes a point where the whole community seems to be under attack ... So people are inclined to go beyond simply looking over their shoulder or keeping themselves down."*

Combat 18 were amongst four right wing paramilitary groups which proudly claimed responsibility for both bombs, which were apparently relatively "rudimentary and crude" devices about the size of a shoe box, packed with nails and other metallic objects. Metropolitan Police Commissioner Sir Paul Condon said the Brixton and Brick Lane attacks - both with crude nail bombs placed in large bags - appeared linked. In addition, several black lawmakers reported receiving threatening letters signed by "White Wolves" - the signature that appeared on a document detailing a bombing campaign that was faxed to a radio station a week before the Brixton incident. The *Sunday Telegraph* said the document stated that all *"non-whites and Jews"* still in Britain by the end of the year would be exterminated. The newspaper said police had dismissed the document as a prank.

Another bomb a week later, this time at a gay pub in another part of London, suggested that this may well have been an unwise decision.

The zealots of the far right were not the only problem that the beleaguered Prime Minister had to face on that balmy Saturday morning.

The previous day, NATO, apparently *"bitter at the failure of their four week bombing campaign, appear to have ditched war time conventions in an attempt to successfully escalate the conflict."*

Desperate to gather momentum toward a land based invasion of Yugoslavia NATO broadened their range of targets. On the 22nd April US military spokesman denied that the bombing of one of Serb leader Slobodan Milosevic's houses, 15 Uzicka Street, in a Belgrade suburb was an assassination attempt. Such activities are expressly prohibited under both US and international law and as such constitute capital war crimes. Neither Milosevic nor his family were injured in the attack which NATO referred to as a 'legitimate target'.

As NATO leaders gathered in Washington, their forces further demonstrated their 'gloves-off' war policy with an attack on a Yugoslav TV station. The bombing which took place overnight killed up to 15 journalists, broadcasters and support staff.

Three days later much-loved UK TV presenter Jill Dando was assassinated outside the front door of her Fulham home, and BBC Chief Executive of News, Tony Hall received a death threat from a caller claiming to represent a Serb death squad.

"We killed Jill Dando. We will kill Tony Hall next," the caller is claimed to have said in a call to the Corporation. The BBC had been criticised for its reporting of the Balkan war. Most criticism had come from the those opposed to the war who complained that its regular bulletins featured a selection of NATO and MoD propaganda briefs. The war in the Balkans, was touted by many as the beginnings of the conflict "predicted" by Nostradamus who wrote:

```
"In the year 1999 and seven months,
a great king of terror will come from the sky".......
```

The war was unsurprisingly unpopular with the public at large who mostly perceived it as expensive, wasteful and pointless. On the morning of April 24th a small gaggle of anti-war protesters were gathered in a lazy group, a figurative stones-throw from the PM`s residence at Number Ten Downing Street exhorting passers by to sign a petition which began:

```
"We the undersigned unequivocally condemn the initia-
tion of war against Yugoslavia, and any compounding
of  this  wrong  by  the  introduction  of  ground
forces......."
```

History doesn`t relate whether it was the presence of the anti war protesters, the threat of attack by Serbian insurgents, or the brooding menace posed by the increasingly belligerent and vicious neo-Nazi groups within the United Kingdom itself that triggered it, or whether (as certain cynical wags of our acquaintance claimed later) that the "People`s Prime Minister" had merely slipped a few percentage points in a public opinion poll, but there was a security alert in London that morning such as had not been seen since the "Ring of Steel" put into place around the Capital a decade earlier to prevent attacks by IRA terrorists.

This was not the right day for three unreasonably cheerful paranormal investigators to be stridently (if untunefully) singing Shane McGowan songs as they drove down Whitehall on their way to the sixth annual *Fortean Times* Unconvention!

The three aforementioned unreasonably cheerful paranormal investigators were myself and my two friends and colleagues Graham Inglis and Richard Freeman. The reason that we were so unreasonably cheerful was that, despite our relative lack of knowledge of the geography of the metropolis, we had managed to negotiate the roads of the capital quite successfully, and we were within only about ten minutes drive of our destination in Kensington High Street. The night before we had set up a makeshift stall containing a motley collection of our own publications, several shelves of second-hand books on a variety of esoteric subjects and a large display of my new book, which we hoped would sell by the figurative bucket load to what was undoubtedly going to be the biggest assemblage of forteans, UFO buffs, folklorists and monster hunters, that would gather together in the same place at the same time in the world during the final year of the second millenium. As we drove gaily along Whitehall, singing *"The Boys of the Old Brigade"* at the top of our voices, we were vaguely aware of two uniformed policemen standing menacingly in the middle of the road, but we were (as far as we knew) breaking none of the laws of the land, and we were blissfully ignorant of what was about to happen.

The larger and more Neanderthal-like of the two `boys in blue` looked straight at us, quickly consulted with his colleague, and raised his hand signalling us to stop. Cheerfully we stopped next to them and obeyed their instructions to turn off the ignition and get out of the car. They asked for our identification and driver`s documents which were perfectly in order. They then subjected Graham, (who had been driving) to a breathalyser test which he passed without a problem. They ordered us to open the boot of the car, and finding nothing more incriminating than a couple of old Batman comics and some rather grubby t-shirts, they then began to examine the car with a thoroughness that I, for one, found somewhat disconcerting.

As far as we knew, the car was perfectly legal. We had checked it only the week before. What we didn`t know, however, was that the tracking of the wheels was awry and that a tiny strip on each of the tyres had been worn away to just below the legal minimum requirement. Resigning my-

self to a fixed penalty fine of £40 and instructions to have the vehicle re-
paired within a period of seven days, I grinned apologetically at the two
policemen.

They glared back at me with menacing frowns. Apparently the situation
was more serious than I had realised.

It was here that I made my big mistake.

I tried to lighten the atmosphere by making a stupid joke. I smiled win-
somely at the younger and least menacing of the two officers and said:

"It's a good job my publisher isn`t here......."

He glared at me, exhibiting no sign of understanding what the hell I was
talking about.

"What do you mean, sir?" he barked interrogatively, obviously suspect-
ing that I was trying to bribe or threaten him, or otherwise pervert the
course of British justice.....

Stupidly I continued........

*"Well, I write books about UFOs, and after all the things in `The X
Files` about Government Conspiracies, I`m sure that he would love to
have a publicity photograph of me surrounded by policemen outside the
entrance to Downing Street! He`d probably claim that it was all a cover-
up of some kind aimed at preventing me revealing the truth about flying
saucers, and that there was a crashed UFO and its occupants hidden in
a secret bunker below Whitehall"......*

The policeman stared back at me.

"Is that so, sir?"

and he gestured to his companion who was muttering into a walkie
talkie. Within minutes another police vehicle, this time a Range Rover
containing another three policemen had driven up, lights flashing, and
my poor beleaguered car was being subjected to yet another rigorous examination. By this time, I for one was getting seriously frightened, and

17

only too aware that we were now nearly an hour late for the convention which for the last six years has been my biggest single annual source of income.

It was, however, too late for appeals of clemency. Luckily we didn`t actually get arrested, but my poor little car had a prohibition order slapped upon it, and despite the fact that I had intended to sell it on our return to Exeter we were ordered (on pain of imprisonment) to have the four tyres replaced, and were told that upon our return to Exeter we should have to either get a brand new MoT certificate or scrap the car.

I looked at Graham with a sinking feeling in my stomach. I had just about enough money left in my bank account to pay for the four new tyres, and if we didn`t make a substantial amount this weekend we were in deep trouble. *"Shit,"* I said. We were well and truly busted.

This was only the beginning of several days of what felt suspiciously like harassment by the forces of law and order. We were stopped on a number of occasions, searched and our vehicle documentation subjected to extraordinary degrees of scrutiny. Never again, I swore to myself, would I make the mistake of attempting to engage in light hearted banter with London`s finest. I had learned my lesson.

It was only a week or so later, after we had returned to Exeter, bought a new car and licked our metaphorical wounds, that I realised the irony. Despite my light-hearted joking, there was a significance to the timing of the first time in my life I had ever had a serious run in with the police. Whereas many UFOlogists have made a career of investigating putative Government cover-ups and links between the military and civil authorities with UFOs and other phenomena, I had never done so - or not until now. And a week after starting my first ever investigation into the shadowy world of the MoD and its involvement (or otherwise) in matters ufological I had been busted. A coincidence? Probably. It depends on which way you look at it.......

CHAPTER ONE

I first met Danny Miles at an obscure North Devon rock festival during the late summer of 1981. In those days I was an innocent and not very streetwise fellow in my early twenties, and I still believed that world peace could be achieved by the ingestion of various noxious substances whilst sitting in muddy fields listening to musical ensembles make whooshing noises on (what seem to me now) to be very primitive monophonic synthesizers.

I was, I believe, watching *Hawkwind* playing a spectacularly inept version of *Master of the Universe*, and like most of the rest of the audience, who were cold, muddy and uncomfortable, pretending that I was enjoying myself whilst in reality I was in dire need of both a lavatory and a nice cup of tea, and totally unwilling to avail myself of the horribly rudimentary versions of either facility that had been laid on for our "comfort" by the euphemistically named "organisers" of the event. About a hundred yards to my right were the serried ranks of the local Hells Angel fraternity who were encamped en masse like an iron clad phalanx of doom. It was only twelve years after Altamont, and even in the bucolic wastelands of rural Devon, they felt that they had something to live up to. Unfortunately, for me at least, they had decided to set up camp immediately between the area where I had set up my tiny tent and parked my car and the main exit, and several of the nastiest and meanest looking of them were patrolling the area armed with pool cues and what I think were hollowed out pickaxe handles that had been filled with molten lead. I was therefore somewhat marooned, and feeling uncomfortable, isolated, alone and more than a little frightened.

Suddenly, in the middle of what appeared to me to be a sea of greasy black leather jackets, emerged a delicate, fey looking figure, wearing an extraordinary array of satins and silks in a variety of peacock colours. It looked for all the world as if one of the gaily coloured inhabitants of one of Arthur Rackham's fairy paintings had suddenly been transported into the middle of a field of leather-clad Neanderthals. The figure tripped gaily towards me, and appeared to my addled brain to be floating like a surreal, and rainbow-hued butterfly above the sea of mud and motorbikes. As it got closer I could see that it was a youth, hardly old enough

19

to shave, with an angelic halo of light brown hair surrounding a face that was covered with intricate paintings of butterflies and lotus flowers. He came and sat next to me and my companions. Much to my amazement everyone else who was with me seemed to take this apparition in their stride. *"`Lo Danny"*, one of them grunted cheerfully, *"`ow are y`doing?"*. Another friend asked him what the hell he had been doing wandering blithely through the middle of the taciturn, unfriendly and potentially dangerous crowd of bikers. *"Ahhhhh they`re harmless."* he said, in an Irish accent that he seemed to be able to turn on and off at will, *"and anyway they wouldn`t hurt me...I am Legion, I am many"*.

His name was Danny Miles, and for reasons known best to himself he had recently adopted the nom-de-guerre of `Legion the Cosmic Dancer`. I got to know him reasonably well over the next few years, and he would occasionally drift into my life, causing chaos for a few weeks and then disappear as simply as he had arrived. During the years when fashions were led by *Culture Club* and the New Romantics, Danny was in his element. He paraded his omnisexuality for all to see like some magnificent, (if slightly deranged) bird of paradise, and flirted outrageously with boys and girls alike. As the decade of Thatcherism advanced and my life became more normal, and I drifted into my disastrous marriage and the twin pitfalls of a job and a mortgage I saw less of him, but he would still turn up once in a while, and we would sit up long into the night drinking wine, gazing at the stars and talking about nothing in particular as I dreamed dreams of my lost youth. Danny never seemed to either grow any older or to settle down. I had last seen him eight years after we had first met at The `Treworgey Tree Fayre` - a legendary rock festival in Cornwall during the summer of 1989. I`d been married for nearly five years by then and had put on a lot of weight and was beginning to write books for a living. Danny looked exactly the same and although he seemed to have ditched his nickname (it was cool, so he said, when no-one had names like that - in the decade that started with the Greenham Common protests and ended with the Poll Tax riots everyone had a stupid hippy name and it wasn`t funny anymore), he was in all other aspects exactly the same. He had taken up with an elderly hippy called Basil (who had once been a pillar of the academic establishment in one of the Red Brick universities of The Midlands, until lysergic acid diethelymide had taken its inevitable toll), and was starting to take an interest in something called The Raelian Society. This, it transpired, was a UFO cult started by France's Claude Vorhilan who calls himself Rael, (an abbrevi-

20

Danny

ated form of Gabriel, the Archangel). The International Raelian Society has turned the 'Burning Bush in the wilderness' into a flying saucer. Rael wrote of his being bathed by five female robots, and has his own rather sinister insignia, a star of David pendant with a Swastika at its centre. He hopes to build a mansion for the old gods (the Elohim) to move into when they land again.

Whether or not Danny actually believed any of this stuff is doubtful, but he seemed to be happy with his new-found chums. After all, they, like the hippies before them, were merely another group of social inadequates that could amuse him, and that he could waste his life happily with. Basil was a slightly different matter. He was the nearest to a proper relationship that I (or anyone else who had ever known him) had seen him be part of. Basil obviously adored him, and Danny was quite happy to be adored, so to a certain extent anyway their needs seemed to compliment each other. Whether or not their relationship was physical, I doubted. It wasn't that Danny was averse to sleeping with people of either sex. It was just that until now he had never seen any need to do so. He was too much in love with himself to be in love with anyone else, and sex (or as he put it *"a few minutes of squelching noises"*) was far secondary in importance to him compared to eating, sleeping, mindless philosophising, amusing conversation, or just plain showing off!

My wife and I left Danny and Basil engaged in an extraordinary dance with some young women dressed up as dryads (perhaps they were dryads - it was that sort of weekend), and went back to our tent, and eventually to our safe little home in suburbia. I wasn't to see him again for nearly a decade.

THE   BLACKDOWN   MYSTERY

Ten years on, on the 10th April 1999, I was sitting in the foyer of the Corn Exchange in Dorchester High Street. In the ten years since the `Treworgey Tree Fayre` I had been through a bitter and acrimonious divorce and at least one nervous breakdown, and I had become a professional writer, TV presenter and paranormal investigator, and together with my friends and colleagues from The Centre for Fortean Zoology I was attending the annual Dorchester UFO Conference in order (mostly) to sell copies of my latest book, *The Rising of the Moon*.

UFO conferences are strange things. I have been to many of them over the years and they can - and do - differ wildly. I have been to ones which leave you feeling dazed, where the clientele are barking mad and the speakers are worse, and I have been to conferences which are about as strange and disturbing as a Vicarage tea party. At a particularly bizarre conference one summer I met a young Welsh bloke who ranted incoherently (and unbelievably) about the crashed UFOs (and alien bodies) that are stored beneath every major RAF base in the country. He was convinced that he was very near to obtaining the ultimate evidence in support of his assertions, by the simple means of jumping over the perimeter fences of these establishments and rushing around wildly taking photographs of everything that he could until he was ejected. We pointed out (quite reasonably we thought), that if the British Government was indeed engaged in a cover-up of these proportions, and that something as momentous as the definitive proof of extra terrestrial life was being covered up by the `old grey buggers of Whitehall`, then surely the `powers that be` would have done something to dissuade him from his actions. At the very least we would be talking about a judicial exclusion-order banning him from the vicinity of all MoD property - they did it to various Peace Protesters in the early 1980`s so they could certainly do it to him - and at the very worst we could envisage something happening to him akin to the infamous incident involving a poisoned umbrella and a Bulgarian dissident back in 1978.

He looked at me with disbelief. How DARE I cast aspersions on his research. I shrugged politely. He stormed off. I forgot about him.

He was soon replaced by someone even more mad, but undeniably better looking (albeit in a somewhat disturbing way). Her name was Faye and she was dressed in what appeared to be a fancy dress ballerina`s costume that had seen better days and which was several sizes too small for her.

Despite the fact that the costume was designed for a schoolgirl and she was a buxom lady in her early forties she would have been an entirely satisfactory addition to the melee of customers milling around the front of our stall had she not been obviously at least three rizlas short of a spliff!

She proceeded to tell me (in a whiney sing-song voice) how she had been abducted (why oh why do the `greys` always insist on abducting deluded hippy women rather than anyone of socio-political import for their explorations and experiments?), by *"creatures from another dimension"* who had implanted her stomach and duodenum with a computer chip to cure her bulimia. She was, she claimed, now perfectly cured. She only made herself sick now in a vain attempt to get rid of her implant!

Although it would have been a great temptation to have bought her a few drinks and then persuaded her to give me an illustrated lecture into the sexual mores of the beings from Zeta Reticuli, I have my moral limits, and she was several light years beyond any of them, so I listened politely and managed to get rid of her as soon as I could.

Now THAT was a BAD UFO Conference. Others are merely dull, but occasionally you attend one that is a joy to go to. One such is the annual Dorchester bash run by veteran British UFOlogists David and Virginia Kingston. It is a place where you get a wide range of sane and interesting speakers, and where the clientele are mostly sane and always pleasant. It is a conference that I am always happy to attend, and indeed it is one of the minor high spots of my year.

I was quite happy then that April morning. I had attended several fascinating talks, drunk several cups of tea and eaten some excellent home-made cake and I was feeling replete with the good things of life, when all of a sudden my past caught up with me.

"Yo, Jon, dude...." said a voice that I vaguely recognised. I looked up, and there was Danny Miles. His hair was shorter, and he had eschewed his rainbow warrior garb of the early 1980s for an outfit of designer sportswear in a distressing shade of lilac, and a baseball cap, but he was still undeniably the quondam Cosmic Dancer. *"Legion... um.. Danny,"* I gasped, totally aghast at seeing him again after all these years. *"What the bloody hell are you doing here?"*

23

As I found out later in the pub just down the road our reunion after so many years was not quite as coincidental as it had at first seemed. In fact it wasn`t a coincidence at all. He had found out that we were going to be there from a notice posted on our web site, and whilst it would be horribly egocentric for me to claim that Danny had followed my career over the years - he hadn`t - but he was aware of who and where I was, and what I was doing. Apparently he and Basil had left the Raelian movement a few years before, becoming disillusioned with all of what he described as the *"Rampant bullshit"* surrounding this particular branch of ufology. In fact, he tended to dismiss the subject as a whole as being surrounded with the unmistakable odour of Bovine excrement - a sentiment with which I had a certain degree of sympathy.

However, it transpired, that Basil was still heavily involved with the weirder and more new age end of the subject, and had joined a local group somewhere in mid Somerset which believed that they were channelling dolphin spirits from the lost city of Atlantis, and using the life energy they gathered to `contact` extra terrestrial beings, whom, they believed were going to make the world a better and a more peaceful place.

"Of course, it's all bloody nonsense", he grinned at me, having, apparently at least, gained a distressing degree of cynicism over the previous ten years, *"but Basil`s into it..."* He smiled disarmingly and pointedly failed to finish his sentence, leaving my wondering whether it was his unwillingness to hurt his long-term companions feelings, or an unwillingness to jeopardise his free access to Basil`s private income (which had been a useful meal-ticket for him for the previous ten years), that had forced him to avoid telling his elderly friend of his doubts about the veracity of his new spiritual path.

"Er, do you buy UFO stories?" he asked me apologetically, finally coming to the point after nearly forty minutes of social small talk. My guard went up. I had heard this opening gambit too many times, and it usually presaged an extraordinary tale of alien abductions and government cover-ups, for which the vendor had not a shred of proof and was demanding an inordinate sum of money. *"Yeah, sometimes,"* I admitted as nonchalantly as I could, *"it depends how good it is....."*

Danny settled back in his chair, took a deep swig out of the drink I had bought him, lit one of my cigarettes, and proceeded to tell me an extraor-

dinary story.

First, he asked me whether I knew the small Somerset town of Welling-ton, and the surrounding countryside. It so happens that I do, having spent many happy hours wandering through the Blackdown Hills in a fruitless search for the big cats which supposedly live there. Whilst not as well known as the `Beasts` of Exmoor and Bodmin (the latter of which I have actually seen, but that is a different story), there is a long history of sightings of mysterious animals in the area.

Wellington is known as the `Gateway to the Blackdowns`. The Black-downs cover a large area in Somerset and Mid Devon and have some of the most beautiful, unspoiled countryside in the area. Wellington is seven miles west of Taunton on the River Tone, set in a wide valley with the Blackdowns to the south and the Brendon Hill to the north. It is eas-ily reached by car being just two miles from the M5 and close to both Tiverton Parkway and Taunton mainline stations.

The town is first recorded in the tenth century as 'Weolingtun', by 1086 it is noted as 'Walintone'. As you approach Wellington the landscape is dominated by the Wellington Monument which stands at 850ft above sea level on the Blackdown Hills and is a prominent landmark for Welling-ton. This slender column was built in the 19th century, work started in 1817 and it was finally completed in 1892. The monument was built in commemoration of the Duke of Wellington to commemorate his famous victory at the battle of Waterloo. The length of time it took to build was due in part to financial problems and also the many changes to the de-sign. It is constructed from ashlar masonry and is of a triangular shape. The reason for this was not as commonly perceived, to represent the bayonet of this period; but merely as an economy drive on materials (although at the time of construction there was an obsession for Egyptian obelisks). This triangular shape gives the monument a strange shape if viewed from certain angles. Its shape distorts at some angles and it ap-pears one dimensional with no great depth, and at others solid and sym-metrical. The plinth at the bottom is actually a wall hiding the three large buttresses which give support to the structure and at the top there is a tri-angular cap stone. The column stands at 175 ft and the width at the base is 15 ft.

You enter the monument through a heavy door on the west side. There are 235 steps that have to be climbed in order to see the spectacular views of the surrounding area. It is dark inside as there is no natural light until you reach the top. Once you have reached the viewing platform there is enough room for three people to stand with three circular port-holes to look through. From here you can see parts of Devon, Exmoor and, if visibility is good, even the Black Mountains in Wales. If you look above, you will see that the inside of the triangular capstone has a large stone weight more than 2 ft across suspended from it, this does the job of securing the cap stone and there are bars for safety below it!

Its most recent cultural association of importance was that it was the site where *The Timelords* aka *The KLF* aka *The Justified Ancients of Mu Mu* aka Jimmy Cauty and Bill Drummond made their low tech video for their surprisingly awful 1988 hit single *Doctorin' the Tardis*. This pair of renegade pop art terrorists have a special place in my heart and have been the soundtrack for many of my adventures. They, however, play no further part in this book and have only been included because of my ca-pricious love for rock and roll minutae, but this anecdote does serve to show how Wellington Monument has achieved semi-iconic status in some quarters.

Wellington is also important from a fortean point of view. As veteran British fortean researchers Janet and Colin Bord recount in *Modern Mysteries of Britain:*

"......lorry-driver Harold Unsworth had the misfor-tune to see the phantom hitch-hiker of the A38 around Wellington (Somerset) on several occasions in 1958. The first meeting was in the early hours of a wet morning. Mr Unsworth picked up a middle-aged man in a light raincoat who had been standing near the Black-bird Inn a mile west of Heatherton Grange. During the four-mile journey to his indicated destination, the passenger spoke of recent road accidents. A few days later, Mr Unsworth came across the same man, again wandering along the A38 with a torch in the middle of the night, and picked him up again. The same thing happened a month later. During these encounters there was nothing to suggest that the man was anything other than a living person. But in November 1958 Mr Unsworth became enlightened as to the true nature of his weird passenger, who he had thought might be men-

The Wellington Monument

*The world's only gothic cryptozoologist
at the Wellington Monument*

Another view of the Wellington Monument

tally ill. He stopped as usual for the hitch-hiker,
who said he needed to collect some cases. Mr Unsworth
waited for him to fetch them, but after twenty min-
utes he gave up and drove on. Three miles along the
road, he saw a torch being waved and in the head-
lights spotted his friend the hitch-hiker. Apprehen-
sive because he did not understand how the man could
have got to this spot, since no other traffic had
passed along the road, Mr Unsworth decided not to
stop. He drove on, whereupon the man threw himself in
front of the lorry. Mr Unsworth stopped and got out,
but there had been no accident - the man was standing
in the road shaking his fist, angry at Mr Unsworth's
refusal to pick him up. Then he turned away and van-
ished. Understandably, Mr Unsworth did not linger
there either. Other drivers on the A38 also reported
encounters with this same phantom hitch-hiker in
1970, and some collided with him, only to find no
body in the road."

The story that Danny had to relate, however, was far more recent, and although equally as frightening, concerned events that, on the surface at least, seemed that they would be easily verifiable from a historical point of view.

"Do you remember that RAF plane that crashed near the Wellington Monument back in 1995?"

Well, it so happened that I did. Vividly.

Back in an earlier incarnation, whilst I was desperately trying to hang on to what I fondly thought of as my mis-spent youth, and also (although this is almost irrelevant to this story) my faltering marriage, I tried terribly hard to forge a career as a slightly avant-garde pop singer. I had an ensemble known as *Jon Downes and the Amphibians from Outer Space* and, billed as the world's only fortean rock band (the name, after all, was taken from a chapter in Francis Hitching's excellent *World Atlas of Mysteries* and we did sing songs about what is vulgarly known as `weird shit`), we made a number of records that very few people bought and played to diminishing audiences throughout the west of England until my wife ran off with one of our keyboard players and we gave up.

One night in 1995, whilst we were on the first leg of what we euphemistically dubbed a `Tour` to `promote` our latest CD we were playing a gig in the middle of nowhere at a pub called the *Merry Harriers* just outside the remote village of Clayhidon on the Somerset/Devon border.

We had enough trouble getting people to come and see the band at the best of times, but this night was, by no means, the best of times, as due to the crash of an RAF aircraft earlier that day, large areas of the Blackdown Hills, including all but one of the little winding lanes leading to our venue for the evening, had been closed down and so our already small audience was diminished further. As I told Danny, all I could remember about the night was that the place had been crawling with policemen and RAF personnel, some of whom were armed, and that even then, I had been surprised by the level of quasi-military activity in the area.

"Well, didn`t you actually wonder WHY there were so many soldiers and police and all that there?" he asked me, staring straight at me interrogatively. *"Do you REALLY think that there would have been such a military presence in the area if they had JUST been protecting the site of a crashed aircraft?"*

..and he wagged his finger at me as he spoke, and I began to realise that I didn`t actually like Danny much anymore.

My initial reaction was to pooh-pooh his story. It was, after all, completely ridiculous. I had no idea how expensive a Harrier Jump-jet was but the cost of each aircraft had to run into tens of millions. If one was to crash under mysterious circumstances then it was quite understandable that the powers that be would be interested in ensuring that well-meaning sensation seekers didn`t pinch vital bits of evidence as souvenirs, and would therefore post troops, RAF police, accident investigators and Gawd knows what all over the area until the matter had been satisfactorily dealt with.

Of course that was the reason. Wasn`t it?

Being both a reasonably polite kind of guy and relatively unassertive in such matters I let Danny ramble on, and despite myself I began to be interested in his story. I have to admit, however, that I wasn`t paying that

The Merry Harriers, Clayhidon

Above L-R
Pete, Jim, Marcus, Lisa, Dave, Natalie, Me
Below Left
L-R Natalie, Me, Lisa

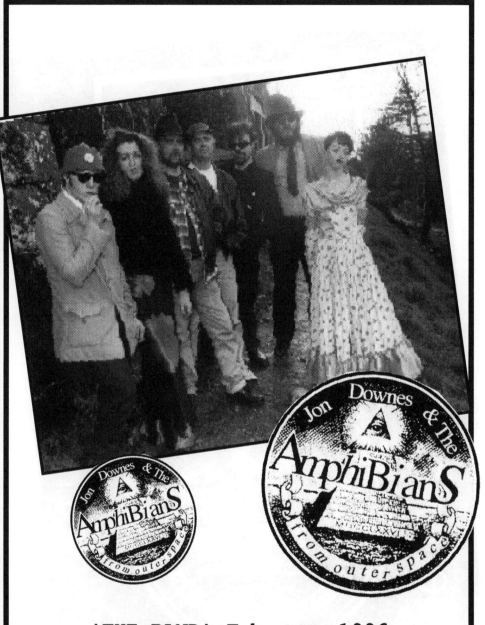

'THE BAND' February 1996

left-right: Jim (keyboards), Natalie (vox), Marcus (bass), Peter (guitar), Dave (drums), Me (vox, guitar, piano), Lisa (vox)

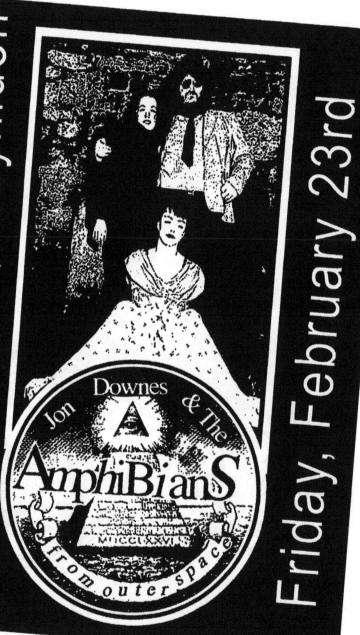

merry harriers, clayhidon

Friday, February 23rd

Jon Downes & The AmphiBianS from outer space

much attention to the early parts of his narrative as I had already dismissed it as hokum, and by the time I had got interested in his tale once again, I had missed large chinks of his narrative (which was, in mitigation delivered in Danny's usual half stoned, and somewhat rambling lisp).

However, the story, as far as I could discern it was this. Danny and Basil were still living in what had been a railway man's hut out in the middle of the Somerset levels, where Basil insisted on living "for spiritual reasons". Although he didn't say as much, I got the impression that Danny was rather disappointed with this decision of his long time partner's. After all, Basil had a reasonable independent income, and could quite happily have afforded to rent, or even buy a comfortable abode somewhere in one of the neighbourhood towns where Danny could then have got on with his favoured occupation of doing as little as possible with undeniable elan and flair.

However, as Basil was the financial mainstay upon which Danny based

The crash site

35

The sighting

his regime of good natured indolence, he could hardly argue with Basil in the matter. However, it was obvious that Danny was finding Basil's increasing eccentricity somewhat irksome, and desired a modicum of financial independence. Selling me this story, was the first step by which this could be achieved.

The story was, in essentials, simple enough. According to Danny, there was a band of renegade new-age travellers who lived in a `park-up` deep in the rolling Blackdown Hills. One of them, an unnamed friend of Basil's had apparently been out upon nefarious business of his own on the night when the Harrier Jump-jet allegedly crashed. Apparently, for several nights before the incident in question there had been huge orange glowing balls of light seen, by many members of his entourage, hovering low in the sky, and on the night in question, they had been there again.

Now, new-age travellers on the whole are quite stoic about such things. Whether this is, (as they would claim) because they are more at one with the fundamental psychic building blocks of the universe because of their anti-materialistic lifestyle, or whether (as many other sectors of society would claim) because they are ripped to the gills on various psychotropic substances for much of the time, and therefore unable to express much surprise at anything, this commentator would rather not speculate. However, it is certain that in any group of a dozen such people one will find at least a dozen (quite possibly or even probably conflicting) quasi-religious or spiritual belief systems, and so I was quite prepared to accept Danny`s assurances that the travellers had taken the appearances of these unearthly glowing balls of plasma very much in their stride. However on this night the scenario was very different. Whereas on previous nights these balls of light had just hung motionless in the sky like huge bioluminescent jellyfish deep in a warm mid-summer sea, on this night Basil`s friend heard the whistling sound of an approaching jet aircraft. There was a bright flash in the sky as if caused by a huge mid-air explosion. The strange thing (said Danny) was that although this unnamed traveller type had seen what appeared to be an explosion, he heard narry a sound, but watched in amazement as something bright fell from the sky to the rolling hills below. It was only then that he heard a dull thud as whatever it was hit the ground on the opposite side of the valley to where the hapless traveller was standing aghast.

According to Danny, the "traveller dude" started to make his way towards the crash site which was illuminated with a dull glow. He claims that he did so in order to see if he could help, but it was more likely (I thought), that bearing in mind the modus operandi of people of this type that I had met before, that he was hoping to be able to steal something before the authorities arrived.

Whatever the reason for his actions, they were to no avail, because, according to Danny, by the time he was even approaching the site where the crashed aircraft, or UFO, or whatever it was still glowed inexorably in the winter's night, the area was surrounded by policemen and soldiers and Basil`s friend found himself ignominiously ordered away from the scene.

That, essentially, was the story, although Danny dressed the whole affair up with far more expressive and florid language, and did his best to try and convince me that the whole affair was something akin to an episode of *The X Files* rather than a fairly dull and routine story.

However, being an impecunious journalist and writer, always on the lookout for new stories with which to earn a crust, I promised, half-heartedly, that I would look into the matter, gave Danny my telephone number, bought him yet another drink, and returned to the Dorchester Corn Exchange and an afternoon of lectures and book selling.

CHAPTER TWO

"What do you mean?", said Graham, mildly irately as he opened a can of beer from my `fridge. "Do you REALLY expect us to go on some wild goose chase based on the ramblings of a cross-dressing drug addict and his elderly schizophrenic boyfriend?"

Richard butted in....*"They`re not exactly the most reliable sources you`ve ever given us are they?"* he spluttered with good humoured disbelief.

We were back at the Centre for Fortean Zoology, (in reality the slightly untidy mid-terraced house in which Richard and I live, and where Graham spends an inordinate amount of his time). The UFO conference had been quite a success from our point of view. We`d made a few quid, and we`d had quite a good time overall. It was only now, as we were unwinding with a few cold beers that I found the courage to tell my intrepid fellow travellers about the adventure that lay before us.

Those of you familiar with my inky fingered scribblings will know about The Centre for Fortean Zoology. Others may be less fortunate. My first love in the field of unexplained mysteries is, was and always has been Cryptozoology - the search for unknown species of animal. When I last left gainful employment during the spring of 1990 I decided that I had spent enough of my life doing things that I didn`t really want to do and that from henceforth I would work at things that actually interested me.

I decided to see whether I could make a living investigating mystery animals and writing about my experiences. I soon found out that, purely as a private individual, I simply couldn`t. There were just too many ordinary folk who were interested in extra-ordinary subjects, and it seemed that the vast majority of them styled themselves as "Investigators" of some order or other. Although many if not all of these people were well meaning and some were particularly knowledgeable on their own particular subjects a small but vociferous minority ranged from the eccentric to the barking mad, and it was somewhat galling whilst on the trail of something like the `Beast of Bodmin` to be accused of being part of the lunatic fringe rather than a bona fide earnest seeker after truth.

One of the problems with all fringe scientific disciplines, is that because of their very nature they have no professional body, and no qualifications to add lustre and credibility to their adherents. I therefore thought, in my Machievellian way, that the most logical way to provide myself with some spurious credibility was to `invent` a professional organisation (with myself as director). In 1992, therefore, my ex-wife and I `founded` the Centre for Fortean Zoology, by the simple means of deciding upon a name and saying that we were it. Seven years later, more by luck than by judgement it had blossomed into an unwieldy if somewhat successful organisation with representatives all over the globe and a series of acclaimed publications.

Graham Inglis became the Deputy Director of the CFZ in the summer of 1996, and since then he has shared in what a character in one of the Billy Bunter books described as *"the wings and sparrows of outrageous fortune"* which seem to beset all fortean investigators. Together he and I have crossed the Puebla desert in central Mexico, scaled rain forest peaks in Puerto Rico and drunk an inordinate amount of alcohol. He is a wiry man in his early forties, whose hair is either close cropped in the manner of one of Britain`s less alluring football hooligans, or worn in an untidy and shaggy mop somewhat reminiscent of an Old English sheepdog on mescaline. He has a beard which comes and goes, and veers between being clean shaven and heavily hirsute. He has a prodigious appetite for beer, Star Trek and the music of *Hawkwind*. He is also the chairman of the local Greenpeace group and is a passionate campaigner against genetically modified foods and the havoc that mankind is determined to wreak upon the earth upon which we live.

Richard Freeman, on the other hand, is a relatively recent addition to the CFZ posse. He started subscribing to our journal *Animals & Men* during 1995, and in the years following my divorce became a close friend to both Graham and myself. He came to live in Exeter during the long, hot summer of 1998, and it was only then that he revealed quite what a peculiar fellow he actually is. He is a Goth - which doesn`t mean that he is a member of the relatively obscure central European tribe which eventually over-ran the Roman Empire, but is, instead, a devotee of a certain group of fashionable young people who revel in wearing black, listening to particularly gloomy bass-guitar driven music and indulging in role-playing games and a taste for flamboyantly gothic literature.

Dear Richard, like all devotees of things gothic, has an imagination that sometimes runs away with him, and he admitted to us rather sheepishly that he had indulged in some ridiculous flights of fancy concerning the true nature of the Centre for Fortean Zoology. I live in a small red-brick housing estate called Holne Court, and before he actually saw the slightly bohemian squalor in which we live, Richard had imagined that Holne Court was a splendid gothic mansion in the wilds of Devonshire surrounded by acres of historic park land. He had imagined Graham and me to be landed gentry with independent incomes that we used to finance all sorts of *Boys Own Paper* style adventures in far-flung parts of the world and pictured himself living in a sort of Jane Austen fantasy land where he would be tantamount to the local squire, and be living as the idiot bastard son of Mr Darcy and Allan Quartermain. The truth, as ever, was far more prosaic and involved a great deal of fairly sordid research into stories like Danny`s which we eventually endeavour to flog around the popular press.

However, even by our standards, the story that Danny had recounted, involving as it did witnesses who were all either barking mad or social undesirables (and usually both) was highly dubious. Richard is somewhat of a cryptozoological purist and secretly resents having to finance pure cryptozoological research by selling UFO stories to the mass media, and although he usually puts up with it with a fair amount of equanimity on this occasion, both Graham and he were adamant that this was a complete waste of time.

"Even if there are such things as UFOs" he blustered, *"and that is highly questionable, why would one choose to crash in the middle of Somerset?"*

"And even if it did," butted in Graham, *"it was four years ago, and all the witnesses we`ve got are bloody hippies who were probably too stoned to know what day it was...."*

But Richard wouldn`t be stopped....

"....and I`m a bloody Zoologist. No, I`m the world`s only GOTHIC Cryptozoologist, ^{TM} and I think....."

41

We never found out what it was that he thought, because at that point the telephone rang. It was Danny with some news for us.

He had managed to locate the hippy who had actually seen the alleged UFO crash. He was still a traveller, and still living somewhere deep in the Blackdown Hills, but was, or so Danny claimed, prepared to co-operate with us in our search for the truth in return for a consideration of some sort.

"I suppose, that's gonna bloody cost us isn't it?" grunted Graham, but we agreed, reluctantly, that if the testimony of this fellow (whose name, by the way was 'Badger'), was any good then we would pay him a cut of any monies we earned from his account. We agreed to meet him at a lonely pub on the A30 a few days later, and then settled down to an evening's drinking and tried to decide what to do next.

It seemed that the first thing we should do was to try and discover the official explanation behind the air-crash, and with that in mind, Richard and I agreed, reluctantly, to spend the next morning poring over back issues of the *Western Morning News* at the Westcountry Studies Library.

The Westcountry Studies Library is a boon for all researchers living in the Exeter area, and it is probably worth quoting from their official website:

"Situated in the Devon Studies Centre, which it shares with the Devon Record Office, the Westcountry Studies Library is the largest local studies library in Devon. It aims to preserve all types of non-archival documentation relating to the four south-western counties and to organise it for information and research at all levels. It originated in the reference library in the Royal Albert Memorial Museum, founded in 1869. The collections largely survived the Blitz of 1942, when the building itself was burnt by an incendiary bomb and they were considerably enlarged when the old Exeter City collections were merged with the County Library's collections on local government reorganisation in 1974."

Such bald prose does not do justice to the treasure trove of information which awaits the earnest writer or researcher who ventures into its hal-

lowed portals in search of information for his or her latest *magnum opus*. It is an invaluable resource and one which I have used on a number of occasions. As well as an unparalleled collection of books, journals and documents on the subject of the four counties of the West Country it also contains a complete collection of the two local newspapers going back well into the 19th century and it was these that we were in search of today.

The problem was that, at this point in time at least, we didn`t really know anything about the case we were meant to be researching. Even my memory of having played a gig in the Blackdown Hills at the same time as the air-crash was no real use because we had played at that particular pub twice that year - once in the autumn and once in the early spring - and I had no recollection of which of these two occasions the crash had occurred. There was nothing to do therefore but go through the newspapers for both periods in the hope that eventually we would get lucky.

Leaving Richard to pore over the microfilms containing the issues of the Exeter Express and Echo for January-April 1995, I started leafing through the back issues of The *Western Morning News* for the same period. After about an hour's work, I discovered something particularly interesting. For such a relatively obscure part of the United Kingdom, and furthermore, one without any great importance either in the Civil Aviation Industry or in terms of the Royal Air Force, there had certainly been a lot of air crashes over the past few years.

The *Western Morning News* for 8th April read:

"Eyewitnesses described the horrifying moment when the Westland EH101 helicopter fell from the sky over East Devon. Simon Neely, 28, said: "The noise seemed very loud. I looked up and saw the helicopter spinning slowly then speeding up again. To he honest, I thought they were messing around - then I saw smoke and realised it was coming down. Three parachutes came floating out and the helicopter continued spiralling down. The pilot seemed to he fighting with it all way the down.

"I think he tried to make it land as safely as he could to avoid the houses in the area. He was a hero there is no doubt about that. When he bailed out, he

was about 1,000 feet. He landed about 50 yards from the wreck Mr Neely was one of the first on the scene and said he found the pilot in good spirits. They were all lucky to be alive," he said. Peter Beigan, 19, was parked in a lay-by on the A303 near to where the helicopter came down. He said he stood shocked and amazed and watched the helicopter fly overhead and then plummet two miles away.

He said: *"1t was like something from a Vietnam movie. The helicopter went overhead and then a loud noise, followed by the helicopter dropping out of the sky in a spiral rotation. The rear rotor blades had slowed down tremendously and just spinned and spinned as it headed to the ground. Then I saw three parachutes appear and this was followed seconds later by a huge bang and popping noise and 1 thought every-one in the area must have been killed"* Another witness, Berry Rumph, said the helicopter looked at first as though it was going to hit his house as it was coming down. He was first alerted by two builders who banged on his patio window.

'1 went outside and thought 'He's low', and the builder said 'Come on, get out, it`s coming down' it was effectively drifting towards us; saw that it was spinning slowly an d then quickly as the pilot tried to control its descent. *"I saw the pilot jump and a few seconds later, the helicopter hit the deck"* Mr Rumph praised the pilot for his bravery in staying with the helicopter until the last few seconds. `I think he deserves thanks from everybody because he did a brilliant job. He had a brilliant sense of humour too. We asked him if he had parachuted before and he said `*No, I think it`s too dangerous*'. Police were last night maintaining a round-the-clock guard of the wreckage as investigations began. The Ministry of Defence and the Civil Aviation Authority were at the scene along with senior Westland executives. Two tonnes of aviation fuel were discharged over the field in the impact. Fireman covered the fuel with foam to prevent it catching fire and pumped water to the site from a hydrant one-and-a-half miles away."

Was there a connection between this incident and the one which Danny

had told us about? My initial reaction was `No` but we had to find out.

Now, Gentle Reader, none of us have ever pretended to be reputable UFOlogists. In fact, if we are gonna be honest about the matter none of us have ever pretended to be any sort of UFOlogists. It is just that due to circumstance it is a role into which we have been thrust on occasion with various degrees of unwillingness on our behalf's.

Richard is a Cryptozoologist, I am a fortean, and Graham is just this seedy looking bloke who, in the words of one of the characters from *A Hitch-hiker`s Guide to the Galaxy* is really *"just this guy, you know"*.

Nick Redfern, however, is a REAL UFOlogist, and furthermore he is actually a good one. A mutual friend of ours, Andy Roberts once said to me that Nick is one of the only people who actually believes (albeit uncertainly) in the ETH (=Extra Terrestrial Hypothesis for those of you interested in such things) who isn`t a complete prick.

In fact, as most people within ufology will testify, Nick is a real *pukka* bloke. He does, however have a slightly dodgy taste in music. Back during the summer of 1977 I was seventeen years old, on the dole and I thought that Johnny Rotten was the next best thing to the messiah. Punk Rock (or so I thought at the time) was a glorious outpouring of violent and arty angst against the system, and its ballsy calls to revolution would have a permanent affect upon the political and artistic zeitgeist of the country. Of course that was bollocks but I was seventeen and knew no better.

Twenty two years later, and it is easy to see with hindsight that punk rock had no long term affects upon either the music industry or the political life of the country. In fact although parts of it were co-opted into the mainstream (Chrissie Hynde - once singer with a distasteful band called *The Moors Murderers* was emblazoned across the front pages of one of the more staid Sunday snoozepapers last weekend, one of The Spice Girls is not just dating the ex guitarist of *The Sex Pistols* but joined him on stage to sing a bowdlerised and buggered about version of `Anarchy in the UK`, and Tony Parsons, the one time punk journalist hired by the NME in 1977 as a `hip young gunslinger` now presents one of the stodgiest and most boring arts review programmes that late night BBC2 has ever come up with and that`s saying something!), most of it was merely forgotten. However for some people the spirit of 1977 is still alive, well and living in Pelsall. His name is Nick Redfern. Whereas most of his peers have gone on to other things, Nick still adores the music of The Sex Pistols and even more so *The Ramones*. He dresses in a moody black, and has a shaved head *("I'll bloody sue you Jon, if you say I'm bald. I ain't bald - it's shaved")* He is also a good friend of the CFZ posse and writes some remarkably good UFO books.

I was still laid low with influenza and was also hoping that Wing Commander X was going to telephone us back. There was some good reason why Graham had to stay in Exeter, (probably to do with the DSS), and so we dispatched Richard up to the Midlands in an attempt to get as much information about the links between RAF crashes and UFOs as he possibly could.

As well as being the *"World's only Gothic Cryptozoologist* ™ *"*, Richard also likes to tell all and sundry that he originally hails from *"God's own Country"* (i.e Yorkshire). In fact he is nothing of the kind. He actually comes from a dull and depressing Midlands conurbation known as Nuneaton. I've never been there, and so can't really comment but to hear Richard talk, it is akin in tediousness to one of the more balls-aching circles of hell as described by Dante or one of his peers. Richard spent three years at university in Leeds, and has used this phase of his life as an excuse to adopt various Yorkshire attributes such as saying "Champion", or "Gradely" rather a lot, and to make extravagant claims about his adopted county.

Very soon after his arrival in Exeter he astonished me by claiming in a loud voice whilst we were shopping in a local supermarket that *"If tha' had charged prices like these in Yorkshire they'd been bloody well stoned to death by t'populace"* and then continued to rant about how the managers of this particular shop were all a bunch of *"southern shandy-drinking shirt-lifters, eeh by Gum"* until Graham and I told him to shut up.

Despite these affectations (which by the way sit ill at ease alongside his trappings of Gothdom, because although Dracula is set in part in the Yorkshire town of Whitby, it is difficult to imagine the Prince of Darkness, Nosferatu or even Nick Cave hailing from North of the Nottingham Coalfields), Richard has never quite been able to rid himself of his Midlands roots, and so when we dispatched him to Walsall to meet Nick

Nick Redfern with some completely imaginary punkettes from his own lurid imagination

Redfern, we did so almost in the guise of a native guide. *"After all"* said

Graham with a grin, as he sat on the end of my bed drinking yet more brandy after having loaded the protesting Gothic Cryptozoologist [TM] ä onto a northbound train, *"he's the only one of us who speaks the right bloody* language".

So, for the next three days, whilst I convalesced, and Graham, having an unprecedented level of access to the CFZ computer either worked on his book about genetically modified foods, or got drunk and played interminable games of *Doom* (he claims the former, whereas I suspect the latter), Richard, the member of the CFZ posse least interested in matters ufological was engaged in a mildly massive (and ever so slightly Gothic) adventure. [1]

The first part of Richard's adventure went completely according to plan. For once the train wasn't late and didn't find itself being diverted care of Cardiff, Liverpool and various locations in the Scottish Highlands. However, when he disembarked at the station in Birmingham where he was supposed to meet Nick Redfern his adventure started for real. Nick was nowhere to be seen.

Richard telephoned me from a `phone box at the station and tried to convince me that (in his words) as UFOs were *"all crap anyway"* things would be much easier for all concerned if he just spent the money I had given him on a *"champion dirty strumpet"* and a *"big meal"*, before he got back on the train to have *"a good sleep"* on the way back to Exeter.

He sounded surprisingly hurt when I replied in the negative.

I told him to telephone me back in five minutes and went downstairs to ask Graham for his advice. He, however, had passed out in front of the computer after a surfeit of *Doom*, lager and *Hawkwind*, and so despite my febrile and delicate condition I found myself having to make the decision upon which the future of this particular investigation would rest. When Richard `phoned back, (still extolling the virtues of his particular

---

1. As, at the time of writing, nearly seven years later, Graham has mastered the computer game, and *still* not finished his book on genetically modified foods - in fact (if we are going to be honest about it) he hasn't actually *started* the damn thing...

plan) I instructed him to get on the bus to Walsall, buy a local paper, find the address of the biggest club in the district which featured punk music, go there and ask for Nick Redfern.

He agreed, but only under protest, but much to his (and, I must admit, my) surprise my obtuse stratagem worked. Apparently, Richard found two clubs situated next to each other.

Manfully ignoring the lure of the Staffordshire Dominatrix Club, he entered the other venue to find a noisily (if enthusiastically) inept musical ensemble making a godawful noise on a makeshift stage in the corner, an audience of mohicaned fashion victims (who weren`t even born when *I wanna sniff some Glue* was banned by the BBC) pogoing up and down in front of them, and a shaven headed, leather clad UFOlogist propping up the bar with a pint of lager.

"Oh Shit" said Nick Redfern with an apologetic grin *"I thought your train didn`t come in for another two hours."*

CHAPTER THREE

Nick and Richard sat at the bar and chatted desultorily as *The Pedo Scat Sluts* finished their set and were replaced by the almost equally inept *Prolapse*.

After an inordinate time spent sitting drinking, chatting and watching mohicaned punk girls bouncing up and down they finally got down to business. It turned out, that as I had suspected there had been quite a long history of links between RAF crashes and apparent UFO reports. Apparently Nick had once interviewed a one-time RAF Sergeant at RAF Boscombe Down.

This Defence Test and Evaluation Organisation (D.T.E.O.) at Boscombe Down in Wiltshire is the MOD's centre for the acceptance testing of all military aircraft and associated equipment intended for use by Britain's Armed Services. It task is to ensure that all aircraft entering service meet up to the standards the RAF require of all the aircraft which it has ordered. The D.T.E.O. is made up of service and civilian work force and is under the leadership of a Commandant, who is an Air Commodore and a civilian Chief Superintendent. It is made up of eight divisions, each headed by a Group Captain or civilian equivalent, supported by administrative services and a small RAF unit. The Empire Test Pilot School (E.T.P.S.) is also part of the D.T.E.O..

It is not surprising that there have been a number of UFO reports associated with this particular base over the years. In 1997 Nick Redfern told The Sunday People about an incident when a small twin-tailed aircraft crash-landed on the runway at RAF Boscombe Down, at about 11 pm on September 26, 1994. Several aviation enthusiasts listening on airband radios drove to the air base next day. They were stopped by police at roadblocks. Before being ushered away, several enthusiasts saw a disabled craft at the end of the runway covered by tarpaulins. Two days later, the wreck was flown to a California military base. Although the craft was initially believed to be a then secret US military plane known as TR-3A, one witness said the crashed craft was completely silent and was able to hover vertically, abilities the TR-3A didn't possess. A month before the crash, a lorry driver reported seeing a UFO over Salisbury. Its description matched that of the crashed craft.

When Nick spoke to Sergeant Rita Hill, she told him that:

"There were always crashes with experimental aircraft. These weren't little biplanes; we're talking about jets and so on. At times we would have a crash a week. I was in charge of a crash crew and had two lads with me. When we went to a crash site, everything had to be found - buttons off the tunics, scraps and so on. Sometimes it would take us weeks to find everything; and from there the wreckage of the planes would be taken to Farnborough for reconstruction.

Well, with UFOs, I'll tell you what I can - but it was all top secret at the time. When the test pilots had finished their tests, they would have briefings, which we would sometimes attend - these were all very hush-hush. Sometimes, the pilots would report seeing strange lights and objects in the sky - they weren't called UFOs at that time. But they would say that when they saw these strange lights, the instruments on the aircraft would go haywire and sometimes the altimeter would just stop! Which is a disaster in itself!

'What the hell was that? What the hell was that light?"' Those are the sort of things we'd hear them say. In these cases, the reports went to Whitehall and we were all sworn to secrecy. It's only now that I've said anything about what I saw." When I finally heard that story three days or so later after Richard`s eventual return to Exeter, I was quite excited because Sergeant Hill`s story was somewhat reminiscent of the account that we had gleaned from The *Western Morning News* about the mysterious crash of the experimental helicopter in the Blackdown Hills in the early months of 1995 and the other episodes of high strangeness that had been reported from the area.

During 1994 there had been a number of UFO reports from the area. Two, taken almost at random from my files are:

June 9 / 23:20 - A woman motorist stopped to watch a horseshoe-shaped object flashing green, orange, blue and red coloured lights as it remained stationary above the Blackdown Hills of Somerset until it moved slowly northwards and out of sight. She had first spotted it hovering between Blagdon Hill and Wellington Monument.

Sept 8 / 03:15 - Three students claimed they saw a
bright bowl-shaped object with something underneath
it, hovering over a road in Taunton, Somerset. The
trio had just watched a video when they heard a hum-
ming, droning sound. The object was reported to be
hovering lower than a church tower and was a bright
luminous white with lights all around it.

However, there have been UFO reports from the region for many years.
A document which is actually in the Public Records Office at Kew contains an account of an official investigation in 1962 by RAF provost and
security services of a particularly interesting incident from that part of
Somerset:

MISS ANNE HENSON, aged 16, said... that on 30th August, 1962 between 10.30 p.m. and 10.55 p.m. she
opened the window of her room which faces N.N.E. and
saw a diminishing star-like object with what appeared
to be red and green coloured flames coming from it.
It was slightly larger than the average star and appeared to be round. After about 2½ minutes it became
very small and she could only see it with the aid of
binoculars. She was quite sure that it was not the
navigation lights of an aircraft because she had seen
these many times and could recognise them immediately. .

She did not look for it again until 17th October
1962, when she saw the object again which was par-
tially obscured by fog. With the aid of binoculars
she compared the object with several stars and noticed that the stars were silvery white whereas the
object was red and green . . . Near to and above the
object she noticed another exactly similar but
smaller object . . She noticed a difference in the
colour of the original object which was now emitting
green and orange flames in the same way as before ...

MRS C. HENSON, mother of MISS ANNE HENSON, said that
she had seen the object described by her daughter.
She could offer no explanation as to the identity of
the object but was of the opinion that it was not a

star. She declined to make a written statement .
[A] visit was made on 1st November, 1962 when the sky
was clear and all stars visible. MISS HENSON, however, said that the object was not in view on this
particular night ... Observations were maintained for
one hour but nothing was seen.

MISS HENSON was asked to continue her observations
and on the next occasion on which she saw the object
or objects to compile a diagram showing its position
in relation to the stars. This she agreed to do.

On 28th November, 1962, the next available opportunity, [the witnesses address] was again visited. However, although observations were maintained for 2
hours the sky remained obscured and nothing was seen.
MISS HENSON was interviewed and said that she had
seen the objects again on two occasions and although
she had compiled a diagram... she had omitted to note
the date. She said that she would again watch for the
objects noting times and dates and compile another
diagram which she will forward by post to this Head-
quarters.

MISS HENSON reports unidentified aerial phenomena and
provides a diagram showing their position in relation
to stars. The objects have not been seen by the Investigator who cannot therefore give an opinion as to
their identity.

It is considered that MISS HENSON is a reasonable
person, although at 16 years of age girls are inclined to be overimaginative. However, MISS HENSON is
supported by her mother, a person of about 50 years
of age, who seems quite sincere. The matter should be
brought to the notice of [the) Department at Air Ministry set up to investigate such phenomena."

Back in 1999, in a spectacularly seedy punk club in the West Midlands
our investigation was going even less smoothly than had the RAF Provost and Security Services` one nearly forty years previously.

Both Richard and Nick were very drunk by this time and the notes which
Richard was taking of the information that Nick was giving him were

sketchy in the extreme./ Richard's handwriting is illegible at the best of times, and from an investigator's point of view these were certainly NOT the best of times. The resulting documentation that Richard brought back to Exeter with him was so difficult to read that I ended up telephoning Nick and getting most of the information that is in this chapter from him down the telephone, thus accomplishing in twenty minutes what Richard and he had singularly failed to do over a period of three days!

However, I digress.

The evening really began to take on a surreal hue when Nick tried to play Richard an interview which he had conducted with the infamous Nick Pole - the man described (by his publicist if by very few others) as *"Britain's answer to Fox Mulder"*. When I first heard this remarkable piece of self-aggrandisement I had never met Senor Pope and was somewhat intrigued.

After all in five or six seasons of the American TV show *The X Files* Fox Mulder (or should we refer to him in future as *"America's answer to Nick Pope"*?) had battled vampires, come within spitting distance of proving that the American Military-Industrial complex was not only aware of an extra-terrestrial menace but was apparently actively colluding with same, tracked monsters, been attacked by strange mutants and had his sister apparently abducted by aliens.

Cool! I thought. If the man being touted as Britain's answer to this televisual hero played with aplomb and flair by actor David Duchovny had experienced half as much high strangeness as his transatlantic counterpart then he was bound to be a hero of remarkable renown.

Of course, he wasn't!

Popey is actually a civil servant. For some years he worked for Secretariat (AS)2a at the British Ministry of Defence during which time he held the rank of Executive Officer. In Pope's own words his old department:

"......provides support to the RAF and works as a link between the RAF on one hand and Defence Ministers on the other, but also assists the public and press. It uses briefings and releases to liase be-

tween the Service
and everyone else" and that when he was working there
he "was aware that UFO research was one of its functions."

From 1991 until 1994, according to his press releases at least, his job
was to assess UFO reports for any possible defence significance. He
found that his predecessor had treated all UFO reports as automatically
mundane and essentially trivial. But Nick claims that, although not a
"believer," he decided to do his job as if the true significance of any
UFO report was actually unknown until studied. What he learned gradu-
ally convinced him that at least some UFOs were most certainly techno-
logical objects of unknown origin, potentially of great significance to the
defence of Great Britain. Though he left the UFO desk in 1994, he still
works for the MoD and now pursues UFO investigations outside his
regular job.

However, then as now, he was a civil servant. He has claimed *that "I
held the rank of Executive Officer when in Sec(AS)2a; this civil service
rank equates to that of an Army Captain. I am now a Higher Executive
officer, which equates to the rank of Major."*

However, as veteran fortean researcher and scourge of the bullshit brigade Kevin McClure has written:

"The comparison with the Army ranks suggested by Mr
Pope did not seem to ring true to me. I had this impression that a Captain could well, in combat, be responsible for the lives and deaths of a substantial
number of men. A Major even more so."

whereas an executive officer

"might supervise up to a dozen staff, but he would
rarely have personal responsibility for significant
decisions involving their deployment. If you get fed
up at your local social security office, or Job-
centre, and demand to see the supervisor, that will
be an EO. It's a job where you need to be honest, accurate, and technically sound, but it's nothing special in the great scheme of things."

Kevin McClure concludes that:

"If the Government has entrusted responsibility for the conduct of its information-gathering, assessment and public relations regarding UFOs to a mere EO, then you can be pretty sure of one of two things. Either it has secrets to protect, and placed in the job someone who has no idea what they are, and whose ignorance is useful in protecting those secrets. Or - and this is far more likely - the Government has long since decided that UFOs have no defence or other significance, and decided to fill its 'UFO liaison' job as cheaply, and as at low a grade, as would be consistent with the rudiments of providing a service to its customers."

I have also investigated the truth behind the assertion that Nick Pope is *"Britain`s answer to Fox Mulder"* and it could, of course, be argued that this is true as Mulder, is of course a fictional character and has therefore never achieved anything. It does seem however as though Nick (actually a rather mild mannered and self-effacing bloke) was actually a fairly low level civil servant whose job for a number of years was to answer the telephone and collect public sightings of UFOs for HM Government.

Nick Redfern has suggested in various public forums that the British Governments UFO research is actually far more serious than either Pope or McClure have accepted, and a few days before meeting Richard told an Internet IRC Channel:

"Nick Pope and I are at this present time at what could be termed loggerheads!!! It is not a personal matter, it simply centres around my belief, based on my investigations, that departments of the British govt and military beyond that in which Nick worked carried out UFO investigations. He does not think this is the case. I do, and that really is the essence of the situation. I suppose the difference is that when Nick and I air our differences, everybody gets to hear about it!"

However, when I had made my initial approach to Nick Redfern for information about `close encounters` between RAF aircraft and unidentified flying whatnots he was kind enough to say that he would hunt out a tape recording of an interview that he had conducted with Popey on this very subject. He had been as good as his word and had brought the tape along to the punk club so that Richard could hear it.

Unfortunately Richard had forgotten to bring a tape recorder with him! Whether this was my cock up in forgetting to give it to him before he left (which is what Richard says) or his cock-up in that he left it on the train (which, considering the undoubted fact that I have not been able to find the damned thing in my house from that day to this, is what I suspect), I have no idea, but Richard and Nick were in somewhat of a quandary at this point until someone (I believe it was the barman - a heavily tattooed skinhead called `Big Mack` - who hopefully had acquired his nickname due to a diet of burgers and fast food rather than for any less salubrious reason) suggested that it would be a reasonably good idea if Nick were to place the cassette into the sound system of the rather seedy little club (a regular staging post for Senor Redfern and his punky pals every Friday night) in which they were sitting.

Assuming, quite naturally, that this would mean that his precious interview would only be audible to the other people sitting at the bar, and would not affect the vast majority of the folk in the club, Nick agreed and handed over the cassette. Imagine the hilarity which ensued (says Richard, who even now can hardly recount the incident without laughing), when due either to a misinterpretation somewhere along the line, or, more likely because Big Mack was as inept as he was drunk, the sounds of an interview with *"Britain`s Answer to Fox Mulder"* were heard by all and sundry blaring out of the clubs PA system, competing with the discordant noises that *Prolapse* were still producing on the stage.

It says quite a lot about the zeitgeist of the British music buying public that no-one really noticed. People have become so used to the idea of rapiers using samples from TV programmes and films over the last few years, that they must have thought that *Prolapse* were making some sort of bizarre post-modernist statement about the function of belief in a contemporary society.

From what I can gather, their singer was so technically and vocally inept that his contribution to the wall of rather unpleasant sound that had washed out over the assembled multitude was rudimentary in the extreme, and according to Richard, the audience, who obviously assumed

58

that Popey was *Prolapse*'s new lead vocalist, were quite happy to continue jumping up and down in some degree of unison with the uncertain
and unsteady rhythm of the drums, and were impervious to the fact that
what they were actually listening to was potentially political dynamite as
Nick Pope described his investigations into a 1970 incident when an
RAF Lightning aircraft crashed in the North Sea, allegedly after an encounter with a UFO.

Nick had been telling Richard an extraordinary story which had first appeared in the pages of the *Grimsby Evening Telegraph*. One evening in
the autumn of 1970 a USAF Officer was killed after his plane crash
landed in the North Sea. Twenty two years later the *Evening Telegraph*
suggested "that, at the time of the 'accident', [he] had
been pursuing a UFO, a pursuit that led, either directly or indirectly, to his death."

Unfortunately, by the editor's own admission most of their information
had come from a source who had insisted on retaining anonymity, but
even so it seemed a compelling story. They published the transcript of
what they claimed had been the last two radio broadcasts received by
ground staff.

The event soon became part of the mythology of British UFOlogy,
though it has to be said that both Nick Pope and Nick Redfern had cast
some doubt on their being any mystery to the incident whatsoever. The
first edition of this book contained a complete transcript of the last words
of the unfortunate pilot, but as we were getting ready to go to press with
this edition we were told that finally the MoD documents concerning the
case had been released, and that these proved without a shadow of doubt
that there had been nothing more than a tragic accident.

Apparently the family of the officer concerned were highly angry and
upset at the allegations of an alien encounter. It is impossible not to sym-
pathise with them, and anxious not to be seen as one of the hordes of
UFOlogical grave robbers, who ghoulishly jump at any excuse to prolif-
erate their loopy theories without thought of the pain that these claims
undoubtedly cause to the families of the deceased, I have omitted these
parts from this new edition.

"Oh, yes, I know about that case."

...droned Britain's answer to Fox Mulder over the incessant dub bass stylings of Prolapse who having got over their initial surprise at their sudden change in lead vocalists were beginning to look as if, for the first time all night, they were actually enjoying themselves...

"What I can tell you is I was approached a couple of years ago by a number of UFO researchers - including Tony Dodd, who had in turn got the story from Pat Otter - who had all suddenly got hold of this story that an RAF Lightning had crashed in the North Sea subsequent to its encounter with an unidentified flying object that it had been vectored on to by Fighter Control. I thought that that was quite an extraordinary story, and did my best to find out the facts. I got in touch with the Flight Safety people, and actually called for the full Board of Inquiry file, which is about four inches thick. That file was classified, as all Board of Inquiry files are. I spent a long, long time going through that file with a fine-tooth comb. I also checked the enclosure numbers to make sure there had been no funny business with anything being removed or crossed out. I felt duty-bound to check, because I knew the allegations would almost certainly surface that there had been some sort of cover-up, and I wasn't getting the full story." [1]

The lead guitarist had apparently broken a string at this point, so Nick was left with just drums and bass as he reiterated the basic story.....

"The basic story was that the Lightning was part of an exercise - a tactical evaluation exercise. It was being vectored on to a Shackleton aircraft, and the aircraft was practising the night-shadowing and shepherding of low-speed targets. That's connected with the sort of job that the Lightning might have to do in an operational situation. So, it was basically on a military exercise. The Lightning pilot reported seeing the

---

1.   I have always been exceedingly unimpressed by claims that the British Government are trying to infiltrate UFOlogy, and that they deny information to UFO researchers. I think that the reason that msot researchers get turned down when they request cooperation or invformation from the powers that be is that they are barking mad, or—to be more generous—that he aforementioned powers that be assume that (because of their interest in flying saicers) that they are going to be barking mad.

lights of the Shackleton, and I think sounded disorientated, and subse-
quently the aircraft crashed into the sea. What I can tell you is, from the
file, there's absolutely no reference to anything UFO-related at all; the
word 'UFO' did not appear once in the file. The phrase 'uncorrelated
target' did not appear. Absolutely no indication at all. So, I honestly
can't tell you where the story started from.'"

Back in 1994, Nick Redfern had been anxious to know whether Popey
thought that the Board of Inquiry file would one day be declassified.
Popey was thoughtful and answered.....

```
"I don't know. I don't see why not. You'd probably
have to ask the Public Record Office about declassi-
fication of Board of Inquiry files. But I can tell
you, I've seen that file; I've been through it. I
have found nothing UFO related at all. It's simply as
one would imagine the story of an aircraft crash is:
a very tragic story of a combination of factors lead-
ing to the aircraft crashing into the sea. Well, when
I got about half. a dozen letters from different re-
searchers, I thought the time had come to pull them
out of the standard correspondence file and open up a
file on this one incident, simply so that everything
was in one place. But all the pressure was coming
from UFO researchers. There were no original docu-
ments to suggest that anything unusual had happened".
```

More by luck than by judgement, *Prolapse* and Britain`s answer to Fox
Mulder finished their performances at almost exactly the same time, to,
(due to the unusual circumstances which had forced them to share the
public limelight on this rainy night in Walsall) a surprisingly hearty
smatter of applause.

After this tour de force anything else that happened that evening would
be perforce an anti-climax. Nick retrieved his cassette tape, and the live
entertainment for the evening having concluded the dulcet sounds of
Whitehall`s Mr Entertainment were unceremoniously replaced by the
more abrasive tones of Johnny Rotten blaring out *Pretty Vacant* over two
decades after the event.

It was time for Nick to go, and it should have been time for Richard to
make his way back down south to bring his findings back to me, still in
bed nursing a bout of `flu and a rapidly diminishing bottle of brandy.

The world`s only gothic cryptozoologist ^{TM}
conducts a financisal transaction

When I told him that I was shoving all this stuff into a book, Nick Red-fern asked me to deny the part about him leaving the punk club attended by a pair of blisteringly attractive mohicanned punkettes. Not surprisingly Richard hadn`t told me any such thing because he was too drunk to remember HOW Nick went home and that all he could remember was the ignominious end to his own evening. Richard ended up becoming involved with a red haired teenage prostitute called `Our Nina` who managed to fleece him of sixty quid without the inconvenience of actually having to sleep with him in any more than the literal sense.

Apparently whilst wending his weary way back towards Birmingham New Street Railway station (leaving the manager of Prolapse desperately trying to contact Nick Pope in attempt to see if he could get him to replace the present incumbent as lead singer) Richard was accosted by a stunningly beautiful lady of the night who made it obvious to him that if he were prepared to expend the sum of sixty quid in her general direction, she would give him the seeing-to of a life time.

The fact that the sixty quid which was at that moment in time residing in the inside pocket of Richard`s leather jacket was actually *mine*, presented The World`s Only Gothic Cryptozoologist ^{TM} with narry a moral qualm. After all he could (and did) pay me back out of his giro the following week.

"I mean, she looked like Daphne out of `Scooby Doo`" he said to me plaintively after his return to Exeter, in an attempt at presenting a case in Extenuation and Mitigation.

They concluded their financial haggling and Richard and `Our Nina` went back to her tawdry little flat after Richard had refused to indulge in a knee trembler behind the main Birmingham Railway Station.

When they finally reached her flat, Richard was appalled at quite how squalid, and indeed sparse it actually was. There was a minimum of furniture, a rickety double bed and a couple of posters for local reggae bands. It turned out that `Our Nina` was a heroin addict and she told Richard that her performance would be much enhanced if she was able to procure a modicum of diamorphine tartrate before affording the World`s Only Gothic Cryptozoologist ^{TM} ä the benefit of her professional expertise.

So she went out, allegedly for ten minutes in order to *"score some scag"* leaving Richard in a heightened state of sexual arousal lying in her bed. She was gone nearly eight hours, and returned early the next morning with a tale of having been arrested on suspicion of possession of a `Class A Listed Substance`. She was bailed and went home, but by the time she got to bed she was too tired and freaked out to function so she and Richard just went to sleep.

They didn`t wake up until the middle of the afternoon by which time the incessant cravings of withdrawal had begun to bite again and `Our Nina` made to leave Richard behind again whilst she went in search of yet more heroin. Richard was wiser this time and insisted on accompanying her, thinking that if he did so he would be able to insist that she returned to her place of residence after her needs were sated, so that his could be likewise dealt with.

It may have been a good idea in theory, but it was a lousy one in practice, as Richard and `Our Nina` traipsed all over her particularly insalubrious district of Birmingham in search of enough heroin to keep the pangs of her habit at bay for another few hours. By the time that she had finally scored, Richard was tired and in a bad temper so they went back to her flat, drank tea, ate fish and chips and went to sleep again.

When the next morning Richard awoke to find a note on the pillow saying *"just gone to buy scag - back soon"* and realised he had been there nearly seventy two hours, spent sixty quid of my money and still hadn`t managed to get a shag he gave the business up as a bad job and caught the next train to Exeter where Graham, me and Toby the dog laughed heartily at his misfortunes.

CHAPTER FOUR

Whilst Richard was busily chasing prostitutes and punk rockers around the black country, Graham and I had been busy. I was still riddled with `flu and brandy but that hadn`t stopped us making a few forays out of the CFZ in search of information.

In the complete absence of any information whatsoever from Wing Commander X we decided that we would have to brave the elements and try and find some information. After three more visits to the Westcountry Studies Library we were beginning to feel mightily confused about the whole affair. We knew that the crash had happened. We had remembered that the crash had happened - we had actually been there at the time. Danny`s witness was also testimony to the fact that a jump jet had crashed in the Blackdown Hills that night. We had spoken to everyone we knew in the area and they had all remembered the incident. Why, therefore, was there no mention whatsoever of it in the local newspapers of the time? This, combined with the complete lack of co-operation from Wing Commander X and his colleagues suggested to us, at least during our wilder flights of fantasy, that something fishy was indeed afoot, and that without realising it my reunion with Danny at Dorchester might well have opened up a far squirmier can of worms than we had otherwise thought.

Although we had been unable to find any newspaper stories about the Harrier crash at Clayhidon, we were able to find out information about similar incidents in the area at the same time. During October the Pilot of a Royal Navy Sea Harrier "escaped when his aircraft exploded in a ball of flame as he was preparing to take off on a test flight" from RNAS Yeovilton in Somerset. According to The *Western Morning News* a number of....

```
"bystanders saw the aircraft taxi to the end of the
runway"
```

as the aircraft prepared for take-off.

```
"As the pilot opened the throttle and let off the
brakes, the aircraft exploded. he escaped alive by
```

ejecting from the cockpit. The plane had been taxied
from a hangar after undergoing routine servicing"

The pilot was lucky enough to escape with minor cuts and bruising.

Only a week or so before an aircraft from another Westcountry air base
had crashed killing two RNAS officers. The *Western Morning News* described the incident in some depth:

"A student pilot and his instructor, both based in
the Westcountry, died yesterday when their Gazelle
training helicopter crashed. A Naval board of inquiry
has been set up to investigate the cause of the accident, which apparently happened when the low flying
helicopter hit power lines and plunged on to a bank
of the River Wye near Chepstow.

Both officers were based at the Royal Navy Air Station at Culdrose, in West Cornwall. They served with
705 Squadron, which provides basic flying training
for trainee pilots. The instructor was named last
night as Lt Timothy Gay (29), from Bournemouth. His
student was Sub. Lt. Guy Chapman, 23, from Salisbury.
They were both single men who lived on the base. Four
Gazelles, which are small two~seater helicopters,
from Culdrose had been taking part in a training exercise at RAF Shawbury, in Shropshire.

They left separately yesterday morning to return to
their home base via RNAS Yeovilton, in Somerset.
Workers in the Livox Quarry at St Arvans, near the
crash site, heard an explosion and ran to help rescue
workers. A quarry spokesman said: "Our staff heard
the helicopter flying low down the river. A few seconds later, they heard an explosion and the helicopter crashed into the river bank"

Again, RNAS Yeovilton. Was a link developing? Or were we merely
getting paranoid. Was it just a coincidence that the ill-fated helicopter's
home base at RNAS Culdrose in Cornwall was, only a few months later
the centre of a UFO story of its own?

On the 29th February, The *Western Morning News* reported that:

"Europe's largest helicopter base at RNAS Culdrose has received numerous phone calls in the last few days from people reporting sightings of UFOs in the skies over West Cornwall. Clearly visible from the high ground to the west of Helston, a long string of white flashing lights have been hanging in the sky, stationary and quite distinct. One local resident reported *`I`ve seen them twice this week always in the early morning light`*.

An investigation by Culdrose has revealed the lights are not from alien space craft but the reflected sunlight from the wind turbines on the Lizard peninsula. A Culdrose spokesman explained yesterday:

`During these fine, sunny mornings, the wind direction has been such that the windmill vanes have been aligned to reflect the sunlight to the north. From a distance the actual windmills are not visible but the flashes of reflected sunlight look like an object in the sky`".

Despite the fact that this official explanation is frighteningly reminiscent of that given by the powers that be to explain certain aspects of the semi-legendary Rendlesham Forest UFO case of 1980, this explanation seems, on the face of it at least, to be a reasonably plausible one.

But was there a cover-up? Were the RNAS stations at Yeovilton and Culdrose somehow linked with a bizarre UFO mystery? Were the various air crashes somehow linked? Probably not. But by this time we would probably have believed anything.

However, as Wing Commander X had STILL not deigned to reply to any of our phone calls except with long drawn out grunts, we were beginning to think that something might be afoot, and in the absence of anything else better to do, we found ourselves in the position of having to do what we had been avoiding for nearly a fortnight. It was time to find the original witness and see if he could shed any light on this mystery.

It was a Tuesday morning when we finally set forth into the Blackdown Hills. Richard had still not returned from his sojourn in the Midlands, and so it was just yours truly, Graham and Toby the Dog who went in search of the man referred to by Danny merely as `Badger`.

Whilst not as peculiar as many of the places that I have explored during my years as a paranormal researcher, Somerset's Blackdown Hills are still fairly strange and bely their pleasant bucolic appearance with an air of brooding menace. For many years there have been reports of mysterious creatures in the area. Only a year before the HTV News service reported:

"Mendip farmers in the county of Somerset organized hunting parties on Thursday April 30 in an effort to flush out and kill the mystery catlike animal, dubbed Monster of the Mendips. The creature, described as resembling a puma, is thought to have been responsible for the deaths of at least ten lambs on hillsides in recent weeks, according to the local news. One witness saw it cross in front of her car just the day before. She claimed it was the size of a border collie, with an upswept tail some 16 inches in length. Another sighting took place on the previous Sunday near Axbridge. The news camera team discovered the remnants of another sheep during filming. Its body had been torn to pieces, leaving only the spinal column and legs."

Apart from my occasional forays into the area on the track of big cats and UFOs (usually the former) my only real knowledge of the Blackdown Hills and the surrounding districts has been during my period as a working musician. As I have explained already in this narrative, we played a few gigs at a pub called *The Merry Harriers* near the village of Clayhidon (most notably on the night when the ill fated Harrier crashed), but we had also played a few shows at a pub with the charmingly bizarre name of *The Holman Clavel* Inn which was situated a few miles from the crash site near a village called Culmhead. Now, I have always had a soft spot for this particular pub, partly because of its peculiar name and partly because the clientele (for a time at least) always seemed to like my particular brand of musical madness. It also happens to be haunted.

The pub is about 600 years old and was once a favourite hostelry for monks on their way to Glastonbury. It has a skittle alley (where we used to perform) and a ghost called 'Charlie'. Knowing nothing about the haunting, guests have been woken in the early hours by the sound of skittles being played, though, of course, the alley is empty and locked at the time. Mysterious and inexplicable crashes have been heard and objects frequently vanish of their own accord. The ghost, which according to veteran ghost hunter Andrew Green, has been "seen only three times since 1970, is that of a monk 'with a long, flowing white robe' standing near a wash basin in one of the bedrooms". Sufficient to say, we never saw the ghost, and the only strange noises that came from the skittle alley that we ever knew of were from us, but it is a nice pub and it was here, during the second week of April, 1999 that we arranged to meet the witness we only knew of as 'Badger'. As we drove through the tiny lanes, newly gay with spring flowers and the bright green leaves of the beech trees we were in high spirits. It seemed that we were indeed on the track of something interesting. The *Fortean Times* Unconvention was only a few days away and we were likely to make a good deal of money there, God was in his heaven, *Hawkwind* was on the stereo, and all was right with the world.

We were actually singing to ourselves as we approached the remote country pub in an unreasonably bullish mood. We were looking forward to a few beers, some congenial company and to renewing our acquaintance with a boozer where we had enjoyed some good times. As we approached the pub we saw, to our dismay we saw a shabby and semi-derelict Ford Transit van parked outside. Leaning against the side of the van was a shabby and semi-derelict hippy accompanied by three shabby and semi-derelict (and very thin) dogs on strings. This, presumably was 'Badger'.

Two things immediately came to mind. The first was the very real probability that Toby would take exception to the presence of three large, fierce and scabby looking dogs. He may be extremely elderly now but he has no circumspection when it involves starting fights with other canids of whom he disapproves. The second was that, even ignoring the real probability that we were only minutes away from starting a loud and bloody dog fight in the car park of the hostelry itself, this was a boozer of which I was inordinately fond, and I did not want to renew my acquaintanceship of a few years before with the pub, its landlord and clientele accompanied by a smelly bloke who looked like a more socially undesirable version of one of the characters from a *Fabulous Furry Freak Brothers* Comic Book c. 1971.

Badger

Much to Graham`s disappointment therefore, I muttered to him that we were going to have to wait for a drink *"because I ain`t going into a pub like this with someone like THAT!"* and as we pulled to a halt, I got out of the car and introduced myself to the shabby and semi-derelict hippy who did, after all, turn out to be `Badger`.

Now, I don`t want anyone to get the wrong idea. I was a hippy for many years, and although I eventually grew out of it I still have a few close friends within hippydom and I have a certain amount of respect for their beliefs and their lifestyle. However, as the years pass fewer and fewer hippies remain true to the original precepts of folk like Jerry Rubin and Abbie Hoffman (let`s face it, Jerry Rubin and Abbie Hoffman didn`t re-

70

main true to the original precepts of folk like Jerry Rubin and Abbie Hoffman), and what was once a true alternative culture has become the demesne of pointless wasters and drug addicts.

Ok, if we are going to be honest about this, even the original precepts of hippydom were far from being unflawed.

- Drugs ain`t good for you,
- Flares ain`t stylish
- and Donovan`s music is pointless, childish, and twee, rather than insightful, innocent and visionary.

However many of the original ideas were pretty good and I have adopted many of them for myself.

However, as the swinging sixties became the swingeing seventies, the empty eighties and the nihilistic nineties, `all you need is love` became largely replaced by two new precepts - `all you need is money` and `all you need is heroin`. The original flower children were also largely replaced by two new groups of hippies, each in their own way as disturbing as the other.

The first group was a canny breed of `new-age` businessmen selling overpriced crystals, tarot cards and ethnic tat to serried legions of gullible acolytes too stupid to think up a belief system of their own and operating in such a moral and spiritual vacuum that they are only too happy to adopt any farrago of quasi mystical horse-shit in a vain attempt to bring meaning to their otherwise pointless existences. Of course, some of these people are perfectly genuine and not only believe in what they do and what they sell, but do their best to help their fellow travellers along the karmic path, but the vast majority of these people are just hard nosed capitalist businessmen who provide nothing of use to society and indeed do exactly the opposite - filling the psyches of a generation of losers with the false hope of a non existent spiritual redemption.

The second group of neo-hippies are equally disturbing. Here the situation is even less clear cut. In 1649, at the close of the English Civil War, The Diggers, an early British anarchist group declared the earth *"a common treasury for all"*. With the trial and execution of King Charles I they considered the land liberated from feudal control. Through peaceful direct action, and pamphlets printed on liberated printing presses, The Diggers encouraged everyone, especially the poor, to colonise and cultivate the commons and the wasteland. Digger activist and pamphleteer, Gerrard Winstanley, identified enclosure (or privatisation) of land as the root of a fundamentally unjust class system: *"so for any to enclose them from its kind, to his own exclusive use, is tantamount to the impoverishment and enslavement of his fellow men"*

Max Beer in his *'History of British Social*ism' applauds the Diggers: *"It was as if all the Peasant Wars of the past had suddenly become articulate."* Since then many hippy activist groups have adopted Winstanley`s original mantle. A group of political hippies in the San Francisco of 1967 adopted the mantle, as have a contemporary British group, and it is they that represent most of what is great and good about the contemporary hippy movement. As it was in 1967, it is still a matter of propaganda and media manipulation as much as anything else. As contemporary activist George Moonlit writes:

"Every battle we fight is a battle for the hearts and minds of other people. The only chance we have of reaching people who haven't yet heard what we've got to say is through the media. We might, with good reason, regard the papers and broadcasters with extreme suspicion, we might feel cheapened and compromised by engaging with them. But the war we're fighting is an information war, and we have to use all the weapons at our disposal. Whether we use the media or not, our opponents will. However just our cause and true our aims, they will use it to demonise and demolish us, unless we fight back."

It is hard to argue with that. In so far as that in many ways I see my job as a writer and fortean investigator as part of the same struggle Moonlit describes, I am still a hippy. However for many people, the hippy movement these days mainly consists of 'The New Age Travellers': a raggletaggle army of New Age Nomads who live in ramshackle trailers and busses, collect social security money, and travel up and down the roads and lay-bys of the British Isles with their dogs, dreadlocks and special brew in search of the next free-festival. It could be (and has been) argued that these folk are merely the spiritual descendants of the Romani or Gypsies but in reality they are no such thing.
Gypsies in Britain are descendants of people who survived an attempt at

genocide in the 16th century. Laws making it a capital crime just to be of Romani ethnicity remained on the statute book for two centuries. The British state and people have never apologised for this, never paid reparations - and why should they? Almost every other European state has behaved in the same way. The 1994 Criminal Justice Act is now recriminalising Gypsies. Despite the recognition that Gypsies constitute a racial group for the purposes of the Race Relations Act 1976, they have persistently suffered discrimination and prejudice from the rest of society. The Criminal Justice and Public Order Act 1994 contains provisions which will reduce the number of authorised Gypsy sites available in an attempt to discourage the nomadic way of life which has been central to the lives of many Gypsies for over five-hundred years. The effect of this legislation will be to worsen the hostility shown towards the Gypsy community. However, the Gypsies or Romani are an ancient people who departed from India in the middle ages and reached England and Western Europe during the sixteenth Century.

However, the genesis of the new age travellers is very different. Gatherings in the open air with music are probably as old as anything human beings have ever done. The `Pop Festival' became a more modern manifestation of people's desire to gather and celebrate. We are social animals. In the late 1960's, they went to Woodstock and the Monterey Festivals by the million. In the UK, the free `Stones in the Park' and the Isle of Wight Festivals saw huge crowds. Alongside the commercial events, `Free Festivals' developed. People became fed up with the exploitation, rules, squalor and general rip-off that so many events came to represent. They discovered something. It is a powerful vision. People lived together, a community sharing possessions, listening to great music, making do, living with their environment, consuming their needs and little else. Parallel to all this, the squatting movement was taking off, and groups such as the `Hyde Park Diggers' were beginning to question land rights.

The Windsor People's Free Festival became an annual event over the August Bank Holiday. As numbers continued to rise, and because of the politics of the situation, in 1974 Thames Valley police eventually acted. Forcibly breaking up the site with much violence and injury. After finding a sense of community and purpose, some for the first time in their lives, many adopted an alternative lifestyle and travelled between events in the `season'. They didn't go `home' in between. You got to choose your neighbours and defeated the alienation that many had felt back in the cities. In 1975, the People's Free Festival was re-established on a disused airfield in Oxfordshire. Over 10,000 people came and for two weeks re-invented the event. The following year however, the bank holiday event died due to much police pressure and days of very heavy rain! The Stonehenge Free Festival had been held at the Summer Solstice since 1974. However, in 1977, numbers suddenly increased and this became the Annual People's Festival. Since then, the numbers involved doubled each successive year. The 1984 festival attracting hundreds of thousands over a six week period.

However, during the middle 1980s the movement, which had always been vociferously politicised came up against its nemesis in the form of the Conservative government under Prime.Minister Margaret Thatcher. In objection to the American Cruise Missiles to be stationed in this country, a peace camp was established at Greenham Common and later at Molesworth. However, in February 1985, `Field Marshall' Heseltine, the then Defence Secretary, sent in huge numbers of troops to evict the three hundred or so people and two goats that had occupied the site as the Rainbow Village for some months.

Although the authorities found all this distressing, there wasn't any specific law effective in dealing with it. So they invented some. In the past, a police force generally felt that their job was done when pushing people over their boundary. Thus merely passing on the 'problem' as they saw it. In the wake of the miners' strike, the police had learned how to act as a national force under unitary direction. In early 1985 the Association of Chief Police Officers successfully sought a High Court injunction to prevent the annual Stonehenge festival, and on the first of June there was a violent clash between police and festival-goers at what has become known in hippy history as `The Battle of the Beanfield'. Kim Sabido, a reporter used to visiting the worlds `hot spots', did an emotional piece-to-camera for ITN as he described the worst police violence that he had ever seen.

"What we - the ITN camera crew and myself as a reporter - have seen in the last 30 minutes here in this field has been some of the most brutal police treatment of people that I've witnessed in my entire career as a journalist. The number of people who have been hit by policemen, who have been clubbed whilst

holding babies in their arms in coaches around this
field, is yet to be counted... There must surely be
an enquiry after what has happened today".

No enquiry was ever held. Neither was any Stonehenge festival from
1985 to the present day. It was the events of the first of June 1985 that
saw the final death knell for much of the hippy movement in this country. Up until 1985, the free festival circuit had provided the economic
backbone of all year round itinerancy. Traditionally the three cardinal
points in the festival circuit were the May bank holiday, the Solstice and
the August bank holiday. Without the need for advertising, festival goers
knew to look out for these dates knowing a festival would be taking
place somewhere. The employment of two bank holidays as specific festival times was designed to allow workers the opportunity of attending a
festival without the inevitable bleary Monday back at work. The number
of festivals in-between these cardinal points also blossomed, giving rise
to the possibility of travelling from one to the other (with choice) over
the entire long summer. By selling crafts, services, performance busking,
tat and assorted gear, Travellers provided themselves with an alternative
economy lending financial viability to an itinerant culture.

According to several commentators evidence suggests that the political
campaign to eradicate festivals was aimed at breaking this economy. A
working party set up by the Department of Health and Social Security
published a report on Itinerant Claimants in March 1986 stating:

"Local offices of the DHSS have experienced increasing problems in dealing with claims from large groups
of nomadic claimants over the past two or three
years. Matters came to a head during the summer of
1985 when several large groups converged on Stonehenge for a festival that had been banned by the authorities. The resulting well-publicised confronta-
tion with the police was said to have disrupted the
normal festival economy and large numbers of claims
to Supplementary Benefit were made."

It is obvious that as soon as they scared away the punters it destroyed the
means of exchange. In the years that followed, the right-wing press made
much of dole-scrounging Travellers, with no acknowledgement that the
engineered break-up of the festival economy was largely responsible.
What happened next is not easy to explain, and so to avoid being accused

75

of any sort of anti-hippy bias I have left it to one of the community's own historians to describe the final downfall of the hippy dream in the UK. Alan Lodge, known to many folk in the hippy community as `Tash` wrote:

"Heroin, the great escape to oblivion, found the younger elements of a fractured community prone to its clutches and its use spread like myxamatosis. Once again Traveller families were forced to vacate sites that became `dirty', further imbalancing the battered communities and creating a split between `clean' and `dirty' sites."

He quotes an old time traveller called Decker Lynn, who still lives in her double-decker bus with her children:

"I don't park on big sites anymore. Heroin is some-thing that breaks up a community because people be-come so self-centred they don't give a damn about their neighbours. So many times people got away with it and there were very few busts for smack. They must know smack is the quickest way to divide a community; united we stand and divided we don't."

As Tash explains, there were other disruptive social forces at work as well:

"The other manifestation of community disruption was the emergence of the so called brew crew. These were mainly angry young Travellers feeding themselves on a diet of special brew and developing a penchant for nihilism, blagging and neighbourly disrespect. Whilst festival culture was healthy, the travelling commu-nity could cope, once broken up however, the commu-nity had problems dealing with the exodus. "

Decker Lynn says.

"To start with it was contained. Every family had its problems but the brew crew was a very small ele-ment around 1986, and very much contained by the families that were around. But there was a large num-ber of angry young people pouring out of the cities

76

with brew and smack and the travelling community
couldn't cope with the numbers."

The so called `brew crew' caused constant disruption for the festivals
still surviving on the decimated circuit and provided an obvious target
for slander-hungry politicians and right-wing media, with the entire
scene regularly painted with the inevitable all inclusive black brush.
What had once been a great and noble social ideal had largely died. All
that was left were the aforementioned `new age capitalists` and a few
grubby bands of junkies and alcoholics; human wastage adrift on the sea
of an increasingly uncaring and hostile society.

Within a few minutes of meeting him it became obvious that `Badger`
was one of the latter.

CHAPTER FIVE

Despite my understanding of, and my sympathy with, the social and economic conditions that had produced people like `Badger` I have a strong dislike of associating with smelly, shambling drug addicts. I find nothing in their life style to impress me and I have always done my best to disassociate myself from them and their kind.

Anxious not to compromise my relationship with the locals at the *Holman Clavel* I politely suggested to him that the pub would probably not allow dogs in, and suggested that we drive off up the road in search of a layby where we could park up and talk about his experience. Graham (disappointed that he was going to be denied his long awaited lunchtime drink) grumpily agreed to my suggestion, and so, we drove off.

Despite my misgivings, however, it did seem as though `Badger` had an interesting story to tell. However, there was little that he could add to what Danny had already told us.

At the time of the crash he had been living in the Blackdown Hills with a group of travellers who were, from what we could gather from his disjointed and not very illuminating description, so far beyond `All you need is love` that they had gone through `All you need is scag` and were somewhere between `All you need is guns` and `All you need is social annihilation`.

This bunch of social degenerates included at least one escaped prisoner and an army deserter, and probably would have been wannabe Charlie Mansons if any of them could have got their heads together to do it. However, starting race wars to trigger Armageddon was not their thing. The occasional armed robbery, lots of car theft and the purveying of substances proscribed under Class A of the Dangerous Drugs Act was far more their bag, and from what I could gather from `Badger` they did it with an aplomb and flair which would have made their vocational guidance counsellors proud of them in the highly unlikely scenario of them actually having such things.

He was rather vague about actually why he had been wandering about the Somerset hills that night, but as far as we could gather he was just wandering around in a daze of opiates when he saw the mysterious light hovering low in the sky above him. Piecing together his incoherent ramblings was incredibly difficult, which is why, although we tape recorded our interview with him, I have not bothered to quote him verbatim, purely in the interests of producing a relatively readable and coherent book. Fifteen pages of *"well, man, er...uh you know"* does not a coherent manuscript make, but as far as we could gather the light was a large, dull orange, pulsating ball of plasma that hovered like a giant jellyfish in the air. It was motionless and emitted a faint glow but as far as he could gather it made no discernible noise.

He described it almost as if it were a living being, and although he didn`t appear to have been afraid of it (this might have been bravado of hindsight but was more likely to have been the stupefying effects of the heroin or whatever other pharmaceuticals he had ingested), he was convinced (or so he told us) that it was aware of his presence and that it was watching him.

He told us that he had been watching it for some time when he heard the sound of an approaching jet aircraft from the other side of the valley. It was only then that the object moved, and, emitting what he described as a high pitched whine like the feedback from an electric guitar it flashed across the sky across the valley where it suddenly increased in size by nearly 150%, glowed brightly and then fell to the ground. It was only then that he realised that the aircraft noise had stopped. He looked across the valley to a hillside where he saw flames, and what appeared to be a crashed aircraft.

This was actually a significantly different story from that which had been told to us by Danny. The original account had made no mention of the high pitched whine nor of the fact that `Badger` had been watching the object hanging motionless in the sky above him for some time before the apparent crash. We asked `Badger` about Danny`s claim that the same (or similar) objects had been seen a lot in the area over the previous few days, but `Badger` was curiously silent on this issue. He claimed that it was the first time that he had ever seen anything like it and that although some of the other people at the Travellers Site had claimed to have seen things in the sky he had never paid much attention to them.As we questioned him in some depth about the relationship between him and the other members of this particular travellers community he began to be strangely evasive, claiming that he had only been with them for a few weeks and hadn't really been part of what had been going on. We assumed that he wanted to distance himself from the criminal and anti social activities that this particular group of social malcontents had carried out. He admitted that one of the travellers at the camp at the time was an escaped prisoner known only as 'Ratty'. He also told us that to the best of his knowledge 'Ratty' had ended up at the Fairmile Road Protest camp made famous by a young man called 'Swampy' who had spent an inordinate amount of time hiding in a tunnel below ground and holding up the construction of the A30.

At least this was a lead that we could possibly use to establish some sort of veracity to what he had told us. To me at least the whole thing was beginning to sound like a page from a post psychedelic version of *The Wind in the Willows* with human moles and characters named 'Ratty' and 'Badger'. However, we had come this far and we were determined to go the whole course.

"What about the armed men that you met at the crash site?" we asked.

"I don't know anything about that" he barked sullenly, and refused to answer any more questions unless we gave him some money. Firstly, as we didn't *have* any money, and secondly because I believed that we had probably got everything out of him that we were going to get out of him, I politely declined, and having made sure that we had a contact telephone number that we could use to get hold of him again we bade him farewell and made our way back to the *Holman Clavel* for a drink.

'Badger' had been unable (or possibly unwilling) to give us any more information about other people who had witnessed these pulsating balls of orange light. he claimed not to know any of the names and present whereabouts of any of the other quondam travellers who may or may not have also seen these objects, and he refused to talk about what he had or had not discovered at the crash site. We were unable, therefore, to confirm or deny Danny's original assertion that 'Badger' had encountered a shadowy group of MoD police or worse armed troops. There was no doubt that there had been a heavy military presence in the hills that night. We had seen them from the window of the band's mini bus as we were negotiating the narrow hill roads to the *Merry Harriers* pub where th'

Amphibs played what was possibly the least successful gig of their career due (in the greater part) to the self same air crash that we were now investigating. However, had `Badger` had an even closer encounter with the forces of law and order and if so, what had actually happened.

During the earlier part of our conversation, probably whilst he was still under the mistaken impression that he was going to be able to get either money or drugs (or possibly both) out of us he had mentioned that he had spoken to a couple of UFO investigators in Bridgewater. He had mentioned the names Sandra and Garfield which sounded for all the world like either a comic strip or a pair of low brow pub entertainers but it was all that we had.

"You don`t really expect me to drive all the way to Bridgewater to look for two people that we don`t even really know if they exist or not do you?" whined Graham

"Yes" I said, and so we finished our pints and went.

Bridgewater is a funny town. It is situated on a long, muddy river estuary and so, although it is technically a seaside town it is actually inland, and although it is undoubtedly a market town it is actually a coastal one, and in my humble opinion it has suffered from a sort of base social confusion for so many years it has never quite decided what it actually is and therefore exists in a state of complete and utter confusion for much of the time.

For a few years during the post punk era of the late 1970s and early 1980s it, like so many other small towns in the south west of England was the centre of a thriving musical community. It had a number of jolly good local bands, several venues and even an arts collective which rejoiced in the unlovely name of `Sheep Worrying`. They published an extremely funny fanzine (also called `Sheep Worrying`) and I believe that they also operated some sort of a record label, although I have to admit that I never heard the results of their labours.

At the time I was heavily involved with similar ventures in the North Devon towns of Bideford and Barnstaple and thus had a certain amount of social and musical intercourse with the folks from `Sheep Worrying`. I became friends with a Bridgewater bloke called Clive, who seemed to have various fingers in various pies. In fact (although this is a pure coincidence and absolutely nothing to do with the story) I met him for the first time at the same tumultuous North Devon Rock festival where I had first met Danny Miles aka `Legion the Cosmic Dancer` but that doesn't really matter. Clive was another bloke that I had vaguely kept in touch with over the years and by 1999 he was working for one of the major London record companies. Don't bother to remember this stuff because after another couple of paragraphs he will go away and will not reappear in this story at all.

However, Clive was the only contact that I had in Bridgewater. He still had a house in the town and spent about three days a week there. Although he worked in London he absolutely loathed the place and spent as much time in Somerset as he could. On our way towards Bridgewater, therefore, we stopped at the Taunton Deane Motorway services on the M5, and I telephoned Clive. Much to my surprise he happened to be in, and I told him my quandary.

Now Clive is one of these marvelously useful people who knows everyone and anyone and therefore I wasn't at all surprised when I asked him if he knew of a pair of UFO investigators called Sandra and Garfield he said that he had vaguely heard of them, and although he was going up to London that evening, if I met him in a bar called *The Rifleman* in about an hour he would see what he could find out for me.

Putting the `phone down I grinned. It was nice to know that some of the people that I had consorted with at rock festivals during my mis-spent youth had actually grown up to be relatively together!

Feeling a little bit more confident about the whole affair, and nourished by several cups of incredibly over priced coffee we drove off towards Bridgewater.

Graham is one of my closest friends and I love him dearly. He has also been an invaluable companion and partner to me on many adventures and investigations but there is no denying that he is a monumentally peculiar chap. He has a dour, monosyllabic sense of humour and suffers fools (especially those within fringe science) especially badly. I still remember with pride how, at one of the first conventions that he attended in a professional capacity he reacted unfavourably when he heard a PA announcement about `Psychic Questing`. he was unreasonably offended *by the concept and spent the rest of the weekend muttering about "Psychic Piffle more like"* under his breath. Even now, four years later he still considers the collective noun for a group of people who claim to have unusual spiritual powers as `A Piffle of Psychics`.

Over the years we have investigated many strange and bizarre occurrences across the globe and whenever Graham is convinced of either:

a. The validity of the investigation from a scientific point of view.
b. That he is eventually going to make some money out of it

or

c. That if neither of the above criteria are met, he will still be able to spend a significant part of the investigation in a convenient public house, drinking Stella Artois and/or playing pool

he is happy and a joy to work with.

If, however he thinks that:

   a.   The story we are investigating is purely the deluded ramblings of a group of self publicising drug addicts

   b.   There is no scientific validity for our investigation whatsoever

   c.   We ain`t got a snowball`s chance in hell of making any money out

of it

   d.   Only a tiny amount of the investigation will be spent partaking of Belgium`s finest and playing pool

or (as in the case of this particular investigation)

   e.   All of the above

then our Graham is not a happy bunny.

On this particular Tuesday, he was one of the unhappiest bunnies that I have ever had the misfortune to encounter.

"This is all complete bollocks isn`t it?"* he grunted grumpily as we drove far too fast up the M5 towards our destination. *"I mean, it was just a bloody air crash, wasn`t it?"

He swerved into the outside lane to overtake a highly unstable looking juggernaut. Much to my consternation (we were doing in excess of 90 m.p.h at the time) he started to roll a cigarette nonchalantly with one hand as his other hand gripped the steering wheel......

"Keep your eyes on the bloody road" I shouted in alarm as I saw what he was doing, but he ignored me and continued with his diatribe......

"Is there any precedent for this sort of story? I mean, I have enough trouble in believing in UFOs at the best of times...but crashing into Harrier jump jets.... yeah right!"

He shrugged his shoulders in a bad tempered manner and swerved back into the middle lane of the M5. Diffidently I started to explain that yes, indeed, there had been along history of reports of such occurrences, although it had to be said that many of them had turned out to have perfectly rational explanations.

As an example, I reached over to the back seat of my little Nissan Bluebird and grabbed my briefcase. Opening it, I shuffled through a thick wodge of grubby photocopies until I found what I was looking for.

"You know Colin Andrews?" I asked, knowing full well that this was one name in the business that Graham was fairly familiar with.

"The crop circle bloke?"

"Yeah....." I said.

Colin Andrews is, in fact, one of the best known crop circle investigators in the world. His official biography from *The UFO Anthology Vol-1* CD-ROM reads:

"Colin Andrews, formerly of Andover, England, was an

Electrical Engineer for over ten years with the British Government. He saw his first Crop Circle in 1983. He founded Circles Phenomenon Research International (C.P.R.I.) later that same year, and soon dedicated himself full-time to deciphering the mystery. In 1989 he co-authored the book Circular Evidence with Pat Delgado, which became an international best- seller.

Colin's ongoing research and investigations continue to take him all over the world. He presents his findings in lectures, on major television and radio programs, and in popular magazines and newspapers world wide."

If you ignore the amusing hyperbole of describing the former chief electrical engineer with the Test Valley Borough Council as an employee of `The British Government`, a claim which is literally true but which (as we have already seen in the case of "Britain`s Fox Mulder") implies without actually saying so that he was involved in shadowy government shenanigans rather than merely a civil servant with a mildly uninteresting job in provincial Hampshire, then one is left with a slightly truer picture of the chap.

During the summer of 1981 Colin`s co-author Pat Delgado first told the British press about some mysterious circular impressions which had appeared in the fields at Cheesefoot Head, Hampshire. Over the next ten years Delgado and Colin Andrews, compiled case studies, interviewed farmers and other witnesses and

photographed the formations from hillsides, from the air, and from close-up. In 1991 they published a book called *Circular Evidence* about which no less a publication as the *Times Literary Supplement* wrote:

"The case for the existence of this phenomena stands well on the unembellished photographic evidence as well as the painstaking attempts at analysis."

The book has been in our personal library in Exeter for four or five years now, and I knew that it was one of the few that Graham had ever taken seriously.

"You mean that Colin Andrews has written about crashed aircraft and

UFOs then?"

asked Graham quizzically. This was obviously a development that he had not foreseen.

"Yup!" I said and started to read him extracts from Andrews` article in a 1988 issue of *Flying Saucer Review*:

"Complete mystery still surrounds the top-secret British Harrier GR5 jump-jet aircraft which, pilot-less, flew on for over 500 miles and eventually crashed into the Atlantic Ocean off the south coast of Ireland on Thursday, October 22, 1987. The machine had taken off from Dunsfold in Surrey on a test flight at 16.59 hrs. with Pilot Humphrey Taylor Scott at the controls. Six minutes later, and with-out any hint of an emergency from its pilot, radio contact was suddenly lost over Wiltshire to the west. The last radio message was a routine one, to air-traffic controllers at the top-secret Boscombe Down Air Force Base near Salisbury, Wiltshire.

Other aircraft were immediately alerted after the loss of radio contact, and an American military transporter made visual contact with the Harrier 90 miles to the west of the south-west tip of Ireland. The transporter was conveniently equipped with video camera, and filmed the Harrier in flight! The aston-ished American crew reported that the jet-fighter had no cockpit canopy, and that its pilot was missing. They shadowed the Harrier for 410 miles, until it fi-nally went down 500 miles out over the Atlantic Ocean."

"Hmmm" frowned Graham, impressed despite himself. During the summer of 1997 he and I had driven around Wiltshire taking as close a look as we were able at the two military installations at Boscombe and Porton Down. They are impressive to say the least, and with only a modicum of imagination it is possible to believe anything could be hidden behind the foreboding barbed wire perimeter fences.

"So, did they ever find the pilot?" he asked in a surprisingly excited voice. I grunted assent and continued to read from Andrews` article:

"Despite a huge search operation, involving aircraft, shipping, life-boats and even mountain-rescue teams in South Wales, no trace of the pilot could be found. Then, on Friday, October 23, a gamekeeper, Mr Ken Pitman, came across the body of an airman lying in a field near the village of Winterbourne Stoke, near Stonehenge, in Wiltshire."

"Well, how did Colin Andrews get involved then?" Graham asked, and leafing through my notes I tried my best to answer him. A crop formation of four circles had appeared in a field at Winterbourne Stoke on August 22nd 1987 - which was coincidentally my twenty eighth birthday. Colin Andrews had flown over the field and photographed the formation soon after its appearance, but, chillingly it turned out, that the luckless pilot had ejected into the very same field.

Andrews describes the scene of the crash in some detail:

"A battery of floodlights cut into the darkened countryside, and surrounded a spot in a field just opposite to the site of our set of "mystery circles" A large gathering of Military Personnel could be seen moving around inside the illuminated area. A parachute lay nearby. In the darkness I could just make out two Army vehicles parked in the corner of that very field where the circles had been found. Whoever was in the vehicles was guarding an inflatable dinghy. For some reason which I cannot explain I had had a strong inner feeling that the finding of the pilot might in some way be associated with the phenomenon of the circles. And I had that feeling even before I heard where the accident had happened. Strangely, therefore, it did not come as a great surprise to me when I heard that the mishap to the pilot had taken place above that very field where the circles had been. It seemed only a confirmation."

Andrews decided, that in his words the most responsible action that he could take would be to contact the Ministry of Defence and inform them of his researches into crop-circles throughout southern Britain as well as in other parts of the world, and explain to them how this incident with the Harrier aircraft troubled him.

"So on November 2, 1987, I telephoned to the Boscombe
Down Air Force Base. They informed me that the Harrier inquiry had now been transferred to Prospect
House in London, and advised me to talk to the man
heading the inquiry, Squadron-Leader Graham Davis. I
rang the telephone number which they had given me,
and was answered by a Sq.-Ldr. Pike, who told me that
Sq. Ldr. Davis was still out on Salisbury Plain con-
ducting his investigations, and that it was he (Sq.-
Ldr. Davis) to whom I should tell what I had to say.

Until that point I had made no mention of the corn-
field circles. I now proceeded to tell Sq.-Ldr. Pike
of our research and of our recent discoveries near
this village of Winterbourne Stoke. He was very interested, and asked me many questions. "How do you
think these circles are formed?" he asked. "What kind
of energy do you suppose is involved?" "Where have
you seen these things?" "Do you know of anybody who
has seen one being formed?" etc., etc.

I explained that I believed the phenomenon was very
rare indeed but nevertheless world-wide, but that
this, the southern part of England, is experiencing a
far higher frequency of reports than any other part
of the entire world. And I concluded: "what I feel to
be significant is that this very field in which four
circles were recently found lies directly below the
area in Space where it seems that this pilot was
taken out of his £13.5 million pounds' worth of Jet-
fighter."

Nick Redfern had already informed me that there were files on the crop
circle phenomenon in the Public Records Office, and his researches had
implied that despite the claims of Britain's Fox Mulder, the British Government were indeed very interested in the subject of UFO research..

Only a few days before Graham's and my fateful trip up the M5 Nick
had issued a press release continuing his latest discoveries about the British Governments involvement in these arcane areas of human knowledge.

With his permission I am quoting this press release in full:

UFOS, THE OFFICIAL SECRETS ACT AND THE JOINT INTELLI-
GENCE COMMITTEE - A BREAKTHROUGH.

Has the British Government ever employed the use of
the Official Secrets Act to silence those implicated
in the UFO subject? To those armchair researchers who
proclaim that such an idea is absurd, I say: 'Think
again`

In my first book, *A Covert Agenda*, I presented clear
evidence via officially-released documents now available at the Public Record Office at Kew, that in both
1953 and 1956 orders were circulated throughout the
RAF warning personnel not to talk about the UFO issue
outside of official channels; however, the records
which had been declassified at the time I wrote the
book did not directly reference the OSA or its poten-
tial use from a ufological perspective. Nevertheless,
I was also able to present the testimony of a number
of individuals (some with media ties) who asserted
that the OSA had been used to keep the truth surrounding UFOs under wraps.

Via a file that I secured only days ago from the PRO,
however, I am now able to prove conclusively that
UFOs and the Official Secrets Act go hand in hand.
Exactly why the Government has chosen to release this
file is a mystery in itself, given that it sharply
contradicts past assertions.

The file in question (titled 'UFO Policy') covers the
period 1958 to 1963 and revolves around UFO investigations undertaken by various Air Ministry departments during that time frame. Contained within the
file is a 6-page document dating from December 1960
and circulated at 'Secret' level throughout the Royal

AUTHOR'S INTERJECTION: Oh Dear Nicholas. When will you people realise that the main reason that Governments `keep information under wraps` is
because they cannot be bothered to cooperate with a bunch of shifty looking
middle aged dudes in long plastic macs. The UFO establishment in general
(but not always in specifics) is comprised of a bunch of anally retentive idiots
with whom no government in its right mind would cooperate.

Air Force. Like earlier papers, it details the proce-
dures to be followed in the event that military radar
operators, RAF pilots, civil pilots or members of the
public should report a
UFO.

Interestingly, however, the paper in question contains two eye-opening revelations. First, it states
that in situations where UFOs were tracked on radar,
any military aircraft in the vicinity were to be diverted from their normal flight `to investigate the
phenomena'. Second, and far more significant, is the
Air Ministry's overwhelming desire to prevent the media and the public learning about such intrusions,
trackings and interceptions. I quote from the paper
in question:

'The Press are never to be given information about
unusual radar sightings. Unauthorised disclosures of
this type will be viewed as offences under the Official Secrets Act.' Although brief in nature, this
document (which remained in use until the formation
of the MoD on 1 April 1964 - how appropriate) makes
it abundantly clear that the UFO issue was indeed
covered by the OSA.

On another - but equally important - matter, the file
in question also makes a very brief reference to a
pre-1959 study of the UFO mystery carried out by none
other than the British Government's Joint Intelli-
gence Committee (JIC)!

Certainly, it has long been recognised that at various times since the late 1940s investigations into
UFO encounters have been undertaken by the Royal Air
Force, the Air Ministry and the Ministry of Defence.
However, the revelation that the JIC also carried out
an investigation more than 40 years ago is of great
significance. Why so?

First, the membership of the JIC includes not just
elite personnel from the MoD, the Treasury and the
Foreign and Commonwealth Office, but also the heads
of MI5, M16 and the Government Communications head-
quarters at Cheltenham - GCHQ!)

Second, the fact that (to my knowledge) no rumours have ever circulated to the effect that the JIC undertook its own UFO investigation programme in the late 1940s or 1950s, is an indication of the level of secrecy that surrounded the project.

The files at the Public Record Office concerning the JIC make no reference to a 1940s/50s UFO investigation; however, I am now actively looking to resolve this issue via several methods and hope ultimately to reveal further findings at a later date. At this stage, the extent to which any of this may have a bearing on the allegations of direct UFO studies undertaken by GCHQ, MI5 and MI6 both decades ago and in the present day, can only be guessed at.

In the light of such incontrovertible documentary evidence, (Nick was kind enough to send me a photocopy of the original document as well) it is, perhaps wise, to take accounts like Colin Andrews` very seriously indeed.

I said as much to Graham, who began to look impressed despite himself. So, grasping the nettle whilst I had the moral advantage, I read Graham the rest of Colin Andrews' statement:

"Later on that same day I received a telephone call from the Ministry of Defence to advise me that my information had been conveyed to Sq.-Ldr. Davis, and that it had also been "conveyed to the Boss". "We will be in touch with you again soon," they said. Nothing further has been heard from the Ministry so far. Meanwhile I have been carrying on with my own investigations and enquiries in and around Winterbourne Stoke, and the information I have obtained confirms that the Harrier changed its course by a few degrees right over the field with the circles, and that the pilot inexplicably left his aircraft at about that point in his flight. He was not ejected by the ejector-seat with which the aircraft was fitted. That remained in the aircraft. An inflatable dinghy left the aircraft with him, as did his main parachute. The main `chute was found in shreds, north of the famous circle of stones; Stonehenge...."

Graham had listened to the whole account in deadly silence, but when I read the final line, (admittedly in a portentous voice redolent with self importance) he burst out laughing.

"Stone---fucking---henge? You are kidding I hope! What do you think this is..Spinal Tap?"

and he started to chant the famous lines from what is probably the best rock music documentary (or should that be ROCKumentary) ever made. *"Oh how they danced, the little children of Stone`enge...."*

and we both laughed, but behind the laughter there was a very genuine interest, because for some years Graham and I have been investigating the more unpleasant aspect of crop circles - a phenomenon which has been largely hi-jacked by the more inane elements of the new-age media and somewhat emasculated in the public eye.

CHAPTER SIX

In south Devon, between the towns of Paignton and Brixham lie Churston Woods. These woods have long been of interest to me because of the sightings of mysterious small carnivores which appear to be a relict population of Beech Martens (a species thought extinct in Britain since the last Ice Age). Fifteen separate witnesses over a six week period in August/September 1996 reported seeing what they described as 'a green faced monkey' running through the woods. Although some of the descriptions were very vague most of them described a tailless animal between four and five feet tall with a flat, olive-green face. Although there are primates with 'green' faces, (for example the olive baboon and some of the west African vervet monkeys), none of these correspond in the slightest to the descriptions of a humanoid or chimp like creature which was seen both swinging through the trees and running through the woods.

There were several complex crop formations in the immediate area and a local researcher called Ed Bicknell found the corpses of three magpies arranged neatly in the middle of the formation. This wasn`t the first time that dead birds had been found in Westcountry crop formations.

Veteran Crop Circle researcher Peter Glastonbury wrote:

"In 1995 I found dead pigeons within three separate crop circle formations in Devon. The formations arrived within weeks of each other:

At Matford Barton, near Exeter, farmer Peter Ash called me to report a ringed circle in one of his fields. He stopped anyone from entering the field until I arrived with colleague Graham Johnson. Inside the circle, near the southern edge, I found the first bird. Examination on site showed that the bird's neck had been badly wrung. The actual head was nowhere to be seen. Several feathers were noted to be strewn around within the lay of the crop. We thought that maybe a fox had lain in wait at the edge of the circle waiting for an unsuspecting victim to fly down to feed on the fallen crop. However, if a fox did do

this to the bird, why did it only take the head and
not the body?"

He went on to describe how, several weeks later he found the remains of
another pigeon in the main circle of a complex pictogram formation by
the Torquay ring road.

"This time there was no body, only fragments.   This
bird had been completely shattered.   Some of the
pieces were intermixed with or under the flow of the
crop, nearly halfway around the circle of barley.   On
the way out of the field I found yet another dead pigeon.   This one was perfectly intact and I could not
see how it had died".

A few days later near Dartington in South Devon he found another crop
formation and in hit was yet another mutilated bird......

....."On the edge of this field I found the last pigeon.   Like the first Torquay bird this was also completely shattered, with pieces spread throughout the
standing crop.   There was no sign of animal tracks
anywhere".

Mutilated animals have been found in conjunction with crop formations
in the United States since December 1974, when a pilot flying over a
pasture in Meeker County, Minnesota, saw a dead heifer. It was lying
inside a perfect circle of bare ground on a snow covered field. The eyes,
left ear, tongue, and part of the lip had been removed with what appeared
to be surgical precision. There were neither footprints nor animal tracks
anywhere around the body and the cuts were completely bloodless.
From the air, the pilot was surprised to see dozens of circles in odd, random patterns spread over several acres of land. This case, researched by
Linda Moulton-Howe is seen by many as one of the classic incidences of
UFO related animal mutilation.

According to Peter Glastonbury, however, there was also a precedent for
these happenings within the United Kingdom:

"1n 1990 an amazing crop formation appeared at Bar-
bury Castle, an Iron-Age hillfort just north of Ave-
bury, England.   Nearby, a castrated horse was found
entangled within a barbed wire fence".

He also described a peculiar occurrence from Canada when, in 1992 a crop formation containing a dead porcupine was found...

```
"The poor animal was a mere one inch (2.5 cm)
thick and had been dragged around the circle,
apparently by the circle-making force.  Porcu-
pines will curl up into a ball when danger
threatens, instead of running away to safety".
```

For years I have been researching not only the links between crop circles and animal mutilations but the links between a whole range of quasi fortean phenomena. Animal mutilations were not the only unpleasant links with crop formations that I had uncovered over the years. During 1997 and 1998 Graham and I had presented a fortnightly radio show on BBC Radio Devon called *Weird about the West*. In the early spring of 1997 Pete Glastonbury was our special guest and we had an amusing and entertaining thirty minutes discussing crop circles. He claimed that various researchers have presented evidence to suggest that the grain from affected plants has actually been genetically adapted in some way leading to a far higher metabolic growth rate We wanted to test this, so as part of the programme we asked whether any of our listeners actually wanted to try an experiment and grow some grain from a crop circle at home. We sent out about ten small packets of oats, and sat back to await results. Two days later I got a telephone call from a worried lady who claimed that she was picking up 'terrible psychic emanations' from the corn seeds. She also claimed that she had experienced similar phenomena causing headaches and a feeling of general illness when she had visited a crop formation last summer.

The same morning I received a telephone call from a colleague who said that he had received unconfirmed reports of a formation one of the first of the year, in a field next to the site of a serious car crash. We are not in the position of trying to make capital (financial or otherwise) out of other people's misery so the names and places have been deliberately withheld. According to Pete Glastonbury, in 1992 at Berry Pomeroy in south Devon, a formation in the shape of a dumbell with scythe attachment appeared in a field of barley. It was the first formation of the year in Devonshire. Shortly afterwards there were three simultaneous motorcycle accidents involving green Kawasakis. In each case the driver was relatively unharmed but the passenger on the pillion was killed. Pete vouched personally for one of these accidents which occurred when the bike in question crashed into his garden wall. He was then contacted by the local BBC TV who filmed a news item entitled *Return of the Creepy Crop-Circles* featuring dripping blood-red letters.

Although as a crop circle researcher of many years standing he wished to play down these more sinister elements which may have nothing to do with the formations themselves - at the time at least we were both agreed that, as firm believers in free speech and dissemination of knowledge, we should publicise such events when they occur.

The weirdness didn't end there however.

During the very first journey I had made after carrying the corn samples which I had sent out, my car engine had suddenly overheated and seized. In 1992 exactly the same thing happened to a Mini Metro owned by Pete Glastonbury. To confound the situation further, last summer, I had been photographing crop circles and on my journey home the self same thing happened to my transit van. A coincidence? I hope so. To make it even stranger, the two incidents involving my vehicles took place on the same stretch of road and within five hundred yards of each other. As I jokingly said at the time I was beginning to wonder whether crop circles should carry a government health warning!

On the face of it therefore it seemed as if Colin Andrews' account provided a new and unpleasant link in the chain which would confirm my loosely held theory of fortean inter-relationships, but as I was to explain to Graham as we finally approached the unattractive outskirts of Bridgewater, the truth, in this case at least, was far from being out there. Unfortunately, as I explained to Graham who appeared to take this new revelation as being conclusive proof that our entire quest was perfectly useless, a further but uncredited article which appeared in a home produced UFO magazine, described the results of the RAF Crash Investigation in some depth.

I read the second document to Graham, who not entirely to my surprise, was showing far more interest in this account than he had in Andrew's story about the crop circles. Apparently several items of equipment and fragments of the aircraft canopy were found roughly distributed along the aircraft's track within 3 nautical miles of the pilot's body. However, an extensive sea search failed to find the aircraft wreckage.

The article claimed quite plausibly that:

"The evidence available showed that the seat harness
had been released, and that the parachute-deployment
rocket of the Martin-Baker Mk. 12H ejection seat had
fired through the canopy The most plausible explanation was that the manual override had been acti-
vated. Three possible causes emerged. First, because Scott`s oxygen hose was found disconnected, the
possibility of hypoxia had to be considered. A
postulated sequence was that, because the hose was
disconnected, Scott became hypoxic and therefore
confused following cockpit depressurisation (one
of the required tests), and tried to eject. If the
seat had failed to fire, Scott might have pulled the
manual override (MOR) handle in a last-ditch attempt to abandon the aircraft."

However at that time there was no evidence to suggest that the seat was
other than serviceable for the flight but nevertheless, all perceived causes
for firing of the manual separation cartridge were examined. It is
claimed, however that this sequence requires a combination of four independent human errors and system failures, to take place and the Accident
Investigation Team considered this explanation to be very unlikely.

The article continues at length and goes on to say that:

"Seat manufacturer Martin-Baker says that the investigation puts forward several hypothetical causes,
and that it "accepts the possibility of one of
these hypothetical scenarios as being the cause of
the accident, but feels that the evidence is such
that no one scenario should be given prominence
over the other. The company statement continues:
"Because pilot safety is our concern, Martin-Baker
has acted independently to eliminate even these remote possibilities. A new link has been introduced to
prevent any possible 'incorrect setting of the MOR
interlock' and a robust guard has been fitted to protect the NOR rod from damage by a foreign object in
the cockpit". Despite the fact that the Mk.10 seats
[the mishap seat was a Mk.12H] have given over ten

99

years trouble-free service and have accumulated millions of flight hours, it has been decided to protect
the MOR linkage on Hawk, Tornado, Harrier and on
other aircraft," says Martin-Baker. The wander lamp
has been removed from the Harrier GR.5, pending modi-
fication of its mounting."

Graham, who is somewhat of a techno-nerd on the quiet, was fascinated
by this technical description, and as I took a brief break to light a cigarette and catch my breath, he bombarded me with technical questions, all
of which I was totally unable to answer.

Like me, however, he was touched by the final paragraphs of the article
which read:

"Recording   an   open   verdict   on   Taylor Scott's
death, coroner John Elgar noted that the wreckage of
Scott's Harrier GR.5, which eventually crashed in the
Atlantic, lay "as deep as the Titanic", and would
probably never be found. Elgar described Scott as a
brave, dedicated, and skilled test pilot, saying "We
in this country are very considerably in his debt".
So, what was labelled as 'one of the most amazing aerial photographs ever` according to the *Daily Ex-
press*, as it featured the unmanned Harrier as viewed
from the US C-5 Galaxy transporter, turns out to be
the last moments of an aircraft whose pilot had   ac-
cidentally   been   killed   in circumstances that
border on the tragic. What though if Taylor Scott's
body had disappeared into the deep depths of the Atlantic, never to be discovered? Feature writers would
have had a field day, and no doubt a UFO connection
would have been offered,   and   compared with aerial mysteries of the past.

As it is, one can clearly appreciate the high levels
of competence shown by the investigating officers who
had   the   painful   task   of   piecing   together   Taylor
Scott's last   moments,   and   deliberating   on scenarios, each of which could have caused the terrible
outcome. For several months there was a mystery, and
now there is none. At the very least however, we
shall remember Taylor Scott, an unsung test pilot,
but whose bravery and dedication was exposed for all

to see. Lest we forget...."

I took a deep breath and gulped down an unexpected outbreak of emotion. My composure was shattered by Graham who grunted:

"So it was all bollocks after all, then", and pointed out that we were now entering Bridgewater.

I would have argued with his succinct conclusion if it wasn`t for the fact that I secretly agreed with him even though I would probably have chosen a slightly more elegant way of saying it, and because I was now entering Bridgewater for the first time in years I had to devote my energies to navigating Graham around what must be one of the most perverse traffic systems ever to have been put into place in a small market town.

I was quite shocked as we drove through the little town. I had not visited Bridgewater for several years, and areas that I remembered as being quite pretty and prosperous were now appearing rather grubby and run-down. However we found the pub, parked the car and went in, and there, leaning against the bar, as good as his word was my old buddy Clive. He was wearing a suit and was somewhat older and greyer than he had been the last time we had met, but he was unquestionably the same would-be entrepreneur I had first met nearly two decades earlier as we both promoted concerts for third rate punk bands. The only difference between us was whereas I had eventually given up, his career in the music business had actually blossomed and he had ended up becoming quite a successful A&R man for one of the country`s up and coming dance music labels.

As Graham sipped a pint of lager, and I swilled down a brandy and coke, we caught up on old times with about five minutes of pointless chit-chat until getting down to business.

Yes, said Clive, he had managed to locate them; well one of them at least. He had not been able to ascertain where Garfield lived, although his description of him (*"a complete bloody lunatic who`ll believe any old rubbish"* and who lived in a bedsit with his three year old son) was not encouraging. However, he did give us a telephone number and address for Sandra, and furthermore he had taken the liberty of telephoning her on our behalf to make arrangements for us to drive over and visit her.

The hour or so that we spent with Sandra was one of the most bizarre episodes in the whole investigation if not in my entire career as a paranormal investigator. I have interviewed peasant farmers in the Mexican desert and policemen in Puerto Rico, but I have never encountered anything quite so odd as the household of this dumpy and unattractive UFO investigator on the outskirts of Bridgewater.

She was in her mid thirties, divorced with no children, and lived with her parents in a small bungalow on the outskirts of Bridgewater. The estate on which she lived was obviously quite a respectable one, and the bungalow in which she and her reprehensible family lived was, from the outside at least, unexceptional.

I suppose that I should have been warned by the working model windmill and the three plaster Dutch girls in the front garden, but I wasn`t and thus I was completely unprepared for what we would find as  we entered Sandra`s house. We were ushered into the sitting room by her mother, a woman of uncertain years who wore far too much makeup and had dyed white blonde hair cut in what I believe is called a page-boy cut, of the sort usually worn by someone at least thirty years younger than her (obviously pensionable) years.

She wore skin tight black leggings which only served to accentuate her over sized and remarkably unattractive buttocks and a strikingly horrible fair isle pullover which included some spectacularly ugly scotty dogs gambolling against a nasty and rather vulgar background.

As she ushered us into what she described as "her lounge" (pronounced Looow - enge in her ugly Middlesex accent), she called to her daughter. Her tone was that which one would expect to be used by a doting mother to a sickly and spoiled infant rather than that of an elderly woman to her middle aged daughter.......

"Sandy dearest.......some of your friends have come to visit" she whined in a voice as sickly sweet as the cheap perfume she wore, and whilst we awaited the advent of the woman we had some to meet, we looked around at the room and marvelled at its expensively tawdry bad taste.

It was quite a sizeable sitting room which if it hadn`t been crammed with every conceivable type of nick-nack could have been a pleasant enough living space. As it was, we felt that we had just entered a vision of one of Dante`s outer rings of hell as decorated by Elvis Presley`s mother. I have spent a lot of my life living near or in seaside resorts and I have often found myself in idle moments wondering who on earth buys blown glass day-glo statuettes of little naked boys pissing in the sea, or china hippo-potami with infantile bulging eyes, spastic grins and messages painted on the side claiming `love me I`m cute`. I need not wonder any more, be-cause the painful truth was self evident.

There must have been an entire cottage industry somewhere within the British Isles manufacturing overpriced vulgar tat for this dreadful woman to buy.

Over the fireplace was a framed piece of embroidery, done in a rough approximation of a Victorian sampler. It read:

> `Two Love Birds built this nest!`

I winced and looked at Graham out of the corner of my eye. I was trying not to laugh but he just sat there dumbstruck with horror. He shot me a pained glance as if to say that he was a respectable *Hawkwind fan* and alcohol abuser, and what the fucking hell was he doing in such an awful place, when the door opened and our hostess with the mostest ushered her plain and dumpy daughter into the room.

This is where things started to get really weird because Sandra answered all of our questions in a lisping mumble that was barely audible, and half the time her obnoxious female parent butted in, either answering for her or, more often than not, talking about something else entirely.

At one point in the conversation this remarkably obtuse and irritating woman got up, wandered across the room to where a dejected looking green budgerigar sat moping in a wire cage and started to sing the theme tune from *East Enders* to the terrified bird in a discordant voice.

All the way through this cataclysmically awful interview I was expecting Graham to do or say something outrageous but to his eternal credit he just sat there looking mortified, and slightly bilious as I tried to get some information out of the woman sitting opposite me.

It turned out that Sandra, together with her friends Garfield and Tezza had, a year or two before, started the Bridgewater UFO, crop-circle research and paranormal mysteries Research organisation or BUFOCRAPMRORG for short. Their only qualifications in the field were an undeniably impressive ability to quote enormous chunks of the dialogue of classic episodes of The X Files to each other and the fact that one of them owned a pair of second hand binoculars.

Her friend Garfield `edited` their newsletter, each issue of which consisted of five or six sheets of single sided A4 paper badly typed and photocopied by Sandra and illustrated with pictures stolen from other people`s books and magazines including my own. It was, she told us proudly, stapled up the side to make it look more like a scientific research paper.

When I first asked Sandra about what she knew about the air crash at Wellington, she proudly passed me an issue of their newsletter which was, by the way, called the BUFOCRAPMRORG Bulletin (sic). This particular issue had a front page story with a headline that read:

"The Blackdown Mystery - The Official Report!! - the Truth is finally (sic) revealed!!!!!!"

I quite liked the title `The Blackdown Mystery` and decided to appropriate it for my own use. I assumed from the title that this article was a précis of the official crash investigation report that we had been trying to obtain from Wing Commander X for so many weeks. It was, however nothing of the sort.

It was credited to `Tezza` and proved to be a wildly hyperbolic, and from what we could gather over-exaggerated, account of the story that we had already received from `Badger`. For the sake of the more sqeamish readers of this book I shall only quote the opening paragraph:

```
"Aliens have landed in Somerset. A RAF plane was
chasing a UFO when it spiraled (sic) out of control
and crashed. The pilot was killed and two witnesses
saw it all happen"
```

Having started badly, the piece got worse, claiming all sorts of appalling Government cover-ups and finally suggesting that the aircraft had actually been shot down by person or persons unknown determined to keep secret the existence of a secret underground base near Yeovil where since the end of the Second World War conspirators, both alien and human had been working together on nefarious and highly secret projects.

It was bad enough when you read this sort of crap being written by folk like the self styled Commander X who claim that the United States is riddled with such underground bases of the new World Order, but to read such drivel written about a place in Somerset beggared belief.

I asked Sandra who the witnesses were but she claimed to have no idea, telling us that we would have to speak to Tezza and Garfield. She then proceeded to tell us how one of their witnesses had reported seeing what she was sure were 'Reptoid' aliens in the middle of the Somerset levels, and how there had been a spate of abductions and even cattle mutilations in the area as well.

At this point her mother, who had been un-naturally quiet for at least five minutes started to sing a song from a Walt Disney cartoon and as illustration began to career about the room with her arms outstretched in the guise of a comedy albatross that (putting two and two together) I can only imagine was one of the main characters in the animated feature film. She then started to chatter excitedly about videos, asking Graham and me whether we liked Walt Disney cartoons (as if we were eight years old).

Sandra's parents

"No, they're crap" said Graham finally reaching the end of his tether, and I just tried to ignore her as I asked her daughter whether it would be possible for us to meet the other two members of her self styled team.

"Oh for fuck's sake do we have to?" Graham muttered under his breath, and I have to admit that I was beginning to wonder whether we were going to gain anything of any value from this ridiculous day. Sandra said that she would see what she could do and waddled off towards the telephone in the hallway whilst her mother started to twitter on about Doris Day movies and Graham and I did our best not to strangle her.

Suddenly there was the sound of a key turning in the lock, and a swarthy

looking bloke who looked like a cartoon child molester entered the room. he was wearing a flat cap of the sort sported by Prince Charles et al (which was two sizes too small for him) and the most vulgar purple shirt and tie combination that I have seen in at least twenty five years.

"Oh daddy, you're home"

Sandra's Mummy and Daddy capering about like cretins

she gushed, suddenly affecting a cloyingly annoying little girl voice. Despite the fact that we were still waiting for Sandra to arrange a meeting with Tezza and Garfield she turned to us and said...

"You're going to have to go now dears, because I'm going to make Daddy and Sandy their tea"

Graham looked like he was either going to be sick or hit her, when Sandra came back into the room and told us that she had arranged for us to meet Garfield and Tezza in a local pub.

Only too happy to put this entire distressing incident behind us we thanked her very much and beat a hasty retreat only to find our hostess blocking the exit and insisting that we kiss her goodbye.

"Bye bye dearies" she gurgled at us in a pseudo infantile manner *"Doo come again"*

and then slammed the door behind us.

"Not if I have anything to say on the fucking matter" ejaculated Graham with a snarl as he grabbed me by the arm and pulled me towards our waiting car.

"What a horrible fucking woman" he gasped with disbelief. *"If you ever make me sit through anything like that again I swear I'll fucking kill you".*

I had a horrible sense of foreboding. The only thing that we knew about Garfield and Tezza was that they were co-founders of BU-FOCRAPMRORG with the daughter of our erstwhile hostess, and this simple fact did not bode well either for their credibility as interviewees or for the likelihood of our having a relatively pleasant end to what had so far been an annoying and frustrating pain in the arse of a day!

CHAPTER SEVEN

Anyone who has read this narrative so far will not be surprised to learn that we eventually met up with Garfield and Tezza in a pub. As Graham and I sat nursing our pints and waiting for them to turn up we ruminated miserably upon the course of the investigation thus far. It seemed that despite all our hard work we had actually got nowhere.

The life of a fortean investigator, especially one who like us, does it for a living and has no other visible means of support, is not an easy one. We depend on results. If we don`t get a story then there is nothing to tell, and although many folk in our field like to fool themselves that they are scientists of one sort or another and that they are pushing back the boundaries of human knowledge, when it comes down to it we are nothing of the sort. Graham, Richard and I are story tellers, and whilst we like to believe that our work has some degree of social or scientific validity our bread and butter comes from telling the stories of our adventures in books, magazines and on television. Of course we want to know whether `the truth is out there` or not, but the bottom line is no results = no story, no story = no wages, and like everyone else in the country we have to eat and pay the mortgage. So, days like this ain`t too much fun.

I sat disconsolately and looked around the pub. It was a dingy and fairly sombre little hostelry, and the clientele, such as they were, looked uniformly miserable. I have written a number of books now in which I have chronicled my ongoing love affair with England. My journeys into fortean landscapes have, in many ways, been merely an excuse for me to pursue this romance, and to continue my search for a land which exists somewhere, if only in my dreams.

Looking around me I saw precious little of the England of my dreams. I think the problem is and always has been that I was not brought up here. As a child in Hong Kong, during the final death throes of an Empire on which the sun was never supposed to set. surrounded by all the magic and splendour of the Orient my family and their peers always spoke of England (with reverence) as `Home`. The books I read portrayed an idyllic home-counties landscape, where magic, mystery and high adventure co-existed in a perfectly logical manner with and within a bucolic landscape, where the local cricket team played on the village green, the village `Bobby` rode a bicycle and there was always honey for tea.

I wouldn`t be surprised if a psycho-analyst would claim that my adult life has always been a search for a version of this landscape. Maybe I have always been looking for an analogue of that land where Rupert the Bear, Biggles, Bulldog Drummond, and Just William live. A place where high strangeness is tempered with middle-class respectability and where the values I had assimilated as a child and the phenomena I had investigated as an adult made some sort of sense. In short, I had always been looking for a place where I felt that I belonged and where I could be happy.

Like all love affairs (at least all of mine), my ongoing romance with England was based on a vision of reality that probably existed largely in my head.

I looked around the pub. There was a third rate Australian soap-opera on the television, and no-one was watching it. The juke box played the latest hit record by some group of anodyne nobodies who would be forgotten in six months, and the front page of the newspaper which lay unread on the table next to me told the story of the latest progress in a war which nobody in the country either wanted or was interested in.

Sellotaped to a pillar in the middle of the room were two posters. One showed a scantily clad woman advertising potato crisps which were guaranteed to clog your arteries with polyunsaturated fats, artificial preservatives and monosodium glutamate, and the other proudly proclaimed that we were now sitting in a drug free zone (something of which at least two of the other punters in the bar seemed blissfully unaware). All my life I had been searching for a vision of the mystical isle of Gramaraye, and here I was engaged on the track of a mystery where at best my informants were deluded idiots, and at worst they were enmeshed in a sordid web of deceit, heroin, prostitution, mental illness and Social Security fraud.

"What the hell was I doing here?" I asked the dog quizzically. Toby looked up at me adoringly (as dogs always do), with sleepy brown eyes, scratched himself, yawned and went back to sleep. I asked the same question of Graham who just shrugged and took another large mouthful of lager. *"I`ve been asking you the same question all day,"* he said.

It was here, in a tawdry little pub on the outskirts of an equally tawdry little town, where, at about six thirty on an overcast day a week or so before the last Bealtaine of the 20th Century that, like all of my love affairs, this one began to go a little sour.

What the hell was I doing here? Why had I wasted the last decade trampling around the world in search of things that nobody else was interested in? Why didn't I just give up and get a proper job? And who the hell were those two weird looking blokes waving at me from the doorway of the saloon bar?

They were of course, Garfield and Tezza.

Gerfield and Tezza

Garfield was an ageing and drab looking bloke with long, greying hair tied back in a ponytail. He wore grubby grey-blue denims, chain-smoked and pushed a wheelchair in which a small, vacant looking child sat uncomfortably. The child had been given a stupid celtic name that I have to admit escapes me, and sat in its pushchair scratching as if it were suffering from scabies. Tezza, on the other hand, was a short plump bloke with

a beard and an unruly shock of curly hair. He was dressed equally untidily, and had a slight speech impediment which meant that whenever he
spoke he sprayed everyone within a couple of feet with saliva. It turned
out (or so I discovered afterwards) that whereas Garfield was unem-
ployed and lived off his state benefits for being a rather inept one parent
family, Tezza eked a living selling highly unlikely erotic stories to spe-
cialist and mildly revolting pornographic magazines. They came over
and introduced themselves, and we soon realised that this part of our day
was likely to be as much of a waste of time as the earlier parts had been,
because whilst Garfield was taciturn, bad tempered and unhelpful, first
impressions at least made us suspect that Tezza was merely barking
mad!

The first thing which was resoundingly obvious was that they each had
an agenda of their own. They had both read my book *The Rising of the
Moon* in which I told the story of an unprecedented series of UFO sightings which took place in South Devon during the summer of 1997, and
whilst Garfield wanted to filibuster me into believing that the group that
they had founded had investigated a Somerset UFO flap of at least equal
and probably far greater significance. All Tezza wanted to know, however, was whether I had really ever met Nick Pope.

Tezza and Garfield

Trying to keep them on the subject of the Blackdown Mystery (by now
the name they had given to the incident we were investigating had stuck
in my mind) was difficult but we did our best.

"Well, yeah" snarled Garfield at me *"I know all there is to know about
that incident"*. He looked at me smugly and lit a cigarette.

"Erm, can you tell us about it please" I asked diffidently.

"Well, I could..." he began reluctantly, *"but I don't want to. I want to
talk about my research"*....... and he handed me a poorly photocopied
piece of paper.

"Read this!" he ordered, so I read it.

Location: Chard, Somerset Date: Late summer 1977
KW, her husband and two young sons, aged seven and
six years were returning home to Chard from Yeovil,
and were approaching Windwhistle Hill, an isolated
area, when they all observed a huge orange light to
their left, which was totally static and very low. KW
describes the object as cigar shaped and 200-300 feet
across and approximately 800-1000 feet above them.
They felt extremely uneasy, and experienced some
strange events which involved feeling some kind of
vibration and a very bright white light all around
and inside their car. They have fragmented memories
of some extremely odd occurrences and after arriving
home they felt there was a time lapse of some sort.
This event was followed several days later with another bizarre incident in the same area, although totally different from the previous one.

I looked at him, waiting for some sort of explanation but none was forth-
coming. I began to ask him for an explanation, or at least some degree of
elucidation, but he just thrust another piece of paper into my hand and
barked *"read this"*

Aug 17 1995 -- A giant triangular-shaped object hovering at tree height over a field frightened a family
of four as they were returning home by car late in
the evening. The incident took place at Butleigh
Wootton, three miles south of Glastonbury, Somerset.
The parents and two children described the object as
having three or four bright red lights upon it and
appearing larger than a Hercules transport aircraft.
Although very nervous, the family stopped their vehicle and watched while it moved slowly and silently
across a field just a short distance away.

"Yes, well this is all very interesting" I began, and was about to ask him
about the 1995 incident at Wellington when he thrust a third piece of paper into my hand and, again, barked at me to read it:

Location: Yetminster, Somerset Date: 4th October 1996

JS was returning home from Yeovil to Leigh, and after
reaching the outskirts of Yetminster he saw a diamond
shaped white light increasing in intensity, on the

left hand side of the road about 80-100 feet away. He
estimated a height of 50-60 feet. At first he thought
it must be the headlights of a car emerging from a
road to his left, but then realised there were no
other roads and the light was emanating from the
field to his left. This light appeared to follow him
for about 400 yds . He felt very apprehensive and
strange during the sighting describing feelings of
being in a 'dream state'. After returning home, he
contacted the police on the morning of 5th October,
and it has been confirmed that there were no helicopters in the area at the time of this sighting. He is
most interested to know whether anyone else witnessed
this object. Please contact BUFORA if this is the
case.

"Oh, so this actually comes from BUFORA files", I said in relief. At
least there was some sort of a handle that I could hang this disparate
amount of totally useless information on. *"Yeah"* he grunted.

"So, do you work with BUFORA then?" I asked, in a desperate attempt
to find out what the heck this unpleasant person was trying to get at.
"No" he said, *"read this"* and thrust the fourth and final piece of paper
into my hand. It contained two reports:

Mar 9/ 1998 -- What at first appeared to be a star
in the southerly night sky suddenly descended to an
estimated height of 5,000 ft, reported three men
travelling by car on the M5 motorway 39 miles from
Exeter, Somerset. [sic] The object displayed three
highly luminescent white lights that were very bright
and in the centre there was a large section of reddish coloured light that pulsated in intensity. The
anomaly was about the size of a jumbo jet. As it
climbed the men described seeing a small kind of yel-
low and orange glowing ball that dropped from the
reddish area of the large formation. The glowing
balls of light shot off at high speed towards the
south and were immediately followed by the triangular
shaped lights. [Source: Dave Dunworth - Skywatch UK]

and

LARGE TRIANGULAR UFO SEEN NEAR FROME, SOMERSET, UK

UFO Roundup: Volume 3, Number 34. Editor: Joseph Trainor

On Tuesday, August 18, 1998, at 5:48 p.m., James M. was walking home from work in Frome, Somerset, UK when he looked up and saw a triangular UFO crossing the sky. "It looked kind of boomerang-shaped and black" and "travelled at the speed of a military jet towards Trowbridge" in Avon. "As an avid aviation fan for many years, I can tell the differences between a MiG-29 and a (Sukhoi) Su-27 from 10,000 feet, so I am not wrong in telling people that what I saw is not an aircraft" currently known to exist. "The weird part is that it moved to the left about 500 yards without turning on its 'nose' and without tipping its 'wings' (banking--J.T.) In fact, it stayed on the same heading as before." According to Bret C., the same UFO was seen by two witnesses in Southwick, a village between Frome and Trowbridge the same evening. (Email Interview)

Garfield took a long, slow drag on his cigarette and looked me straight in the eyes. *"What about all that then?"* he said with what approximated as a smile. *"Doesn`t this lot prove that something is really going on?"* and he leaned back in his chair, folded his arms and waited for a reply.

"What do you mean?" I asked nervously *"You`ve got five reports of markedly different objects over a period of twenty one years and they are not even in the same part of Somerset. What are you trying to prove?"*

"You fucking sceptics are all the same", he snarled at me with amazing vehemence. *"you`re just trying to cover up our findings. BUFOCRAPMROG won`t forget this!"* and he rose to his feet and made to storm off.

Graham then demonstrated the qualities that have made him an essential part of my travels and adventures over the past few years. He doesn`t say much, and I know that quite a few people who have encountered the CFZ posse have wondered who he is, and what he is doing with us. Richard and I are both voluble and expressive, and exhibit a reasonable knowledge of the subjects with which we deal. Graham, on the other hand, spends much of the time sitting quietly in the corner taking everything in but not saying anything. When he does say something one knows that it is either going to be a totally mindless irrelevance or, as in this case, something that will literally and figuratively save the day.

"Look. Isn`t anyone going to talk about this bloody Harrier crash, or can we all go home?"

and much to my surprise, considering the appallingly aggressive attitude that he had exhibited earlier in the conversation Garfield calmed down and began to leaf through his brief case in search of the documents that he had which related to the incident.

I breathed an audible sigh of relief and was beginning to think that we were actually getting somewhere when Tezza started to speak for the first time.

For several years between my last proper job as a nurse for the Mentally Handicapped (or people with learning disabilities as we are now supposed to call them) and the time when my career as a chronicler of things fortean really began to take off, I worked on the outskirts of the music industry. I worked as a journalist editing several music magazines, and my ex-wife and I also ran fan clubs for several well known artistes. I have toured with several bands latterly as guitarist and singer and formerly as the bloke who sold the T Shirts and I have spent many years hanging around in bars with people who are reasonably famous.

As an adolescent and later as a young man I was fairly star struck and all I ever wanted to do for many years was to achieve fame and fortune as a rock singer. This was something that I singularly failed to do, but for many years I enjoyed vicarious fame by hanging out with people who were far more famous than I.

Most of my heroes are dead and I have been unlucky enough to work with most of the rest in some capacity or other with the unfortunate affect that now, as I approach my fortieth birthday I no longer have any heroes. When I did, however they achieved a mythic almost demi-God status within my adolescent psyche.

In recent years I have written a number of books, appeared on a number

of television programmes and achieved a modicum of fame in my own right but I never thought that I would be anybody's hero.

Much to my horror it turned out that that was exactly what I had become.

One of the high spots of my career as a music journalist was the day when I sat on the tailgate of my Transit Van and interviewed John Paul Jones, the one time bass player with *Led Zeppe*lin. It was excruciatingly hard to ask him intelligent questions when the only thing going through my head was that I was sitting only a few feet away from the man who had played the `**Bom..ba...Bom Bom Bom**` bass pattern at the beginning of `*Dazed and Confused*` - the song which had been the soundtrack as I lost my virginity.

It seems that Tezza was going through similar emotions. Although I sincerely hope that my writings had not played any significant part in the development of his sex life, it seems that what I had taken as incipient simple mindedness on his behalf was actually him gazing at me with awe as he summoned up courage to ask me to autograph a copy of *The Rising of the Moon* for him.

It turned out that both he and Garfield had read and re-read the book, and although they had totally missed the point of what I and my co-author had been trying to say, they had both enjoyed my book immensely and had been inspired to style their own investigations on my own peculiar modus operandi.

It has always been my contention that what is vulgarly known as `weird shit` happens in waves, and whilst I am not denying either that extra terrestrials may in fact exist or that there is no doubt that a great deal of UFOs are secret military aircraft, I have always seen a link between many UFO reports and reports of other paranormal phenomena. I think that this was one of the reasons that despite myself I found myself getting intrigued with the Blackdown Mystery.

There is no doubt that this particular corner of Somerset has been the epicentre of episodes of high strangeness for many years. As well as the incidents already recounted in this book involving mystery cats, phantom hitch-hikers and UFOs, there have been accounts of dragons, alien abductions, crop-circles, ghosts and strange monsters.

There have even been accounts of Bigfoot type entities such as the accounts recounted by Janet and Colin Bord from a man who later in Africa had a reputation as a big game hunter. He saw a creature at the Hangly Cleeve barrows in Somerset which he described long after the sighting as the most terrifying thing he had ever seen. He described it as a `crouching form like a rock with matted hair all over it and pale, flat eyes`. We have other reports from that area of hulking man shaped shadows that are seen in a local quarry, and my researches have led me to the conclusion that all of these phenomena are somehow connected.

In *The Rising of the Moon* I had analysed these links and hypothesised that they were all created by quasi independent pockets of Odylic Life Force Energy which acted on the human psyche to create these grotesque monsters and strange phenomena. However, although I was reasonably sure that my theory was basically correct I was still desperately searching for new pieces that I could fit into the jigsaw, and in particular evidence of the actual physicality of some of these phenomena. When I was told about what appeared on the surface of it to be a crash between a UFO and an aircraft in a part of the country which has not only been a hotbed of strangeness for centuries, but even according to legend, was visited by Jesus Christ Himself whilst a youth, then I found the possibility that at last I might be on the track of actual physical evidence to support my theory too much to resist.

After I signed Tezza`s copy of *The Rising of the Moon* and whilst Graham went back to his pint, Toby continued to sleep and Garfield was still rummaging in his brief case for his documents on the Blackdown Mystery, I tried to explain the spiritual and intellectual quest on which I was engaged to Tezza.

He gazed blankly at me for a few moments after I had finished and then said:

"But it is all a conspiracy innit? What about Roswell?"

and I found myself wondering how, if indeed Tezza had read my most recent book had he understood any of what I was trying to say, or had he just been seduced by the word UFO in the subtitle and the picture of the Adamski style flying saucer on the cover?

I was just about to try and explain that although I was sure that something had crashed in the New Mexico desert during the summer of 1947, I had no idea what it was and that it had very little (if anything) to do with the events that I had described in *The Rising of the Moon* when Garfield emerged from the labyrinthine depths of his brief case and announced in triumph....

"`ere I`ve got it" and proceeded to tell us all that he knew about the Blackdown Mystery.

By this time, made bold by the fact that I had actually deigned to sign his copy of my latest book, Tezza repeatedly interrupted Garfield`s account and it was very difficult to actually find out what had happened.

"Well, as you can see from the papers that I showed you" he began portentously, *"we have been having a UFO wave in Somerset very similar to the one you wrote about from 1997".......*

I bit back my first reposte which was to repeat that five incidents over a period of twenty two years cannot really compare with over a hundred witnesses in a period of seven weeks and let him continue......

"It's taken us a good deal of research to get hold of all this information, and I feel that you should really take these accounts seriously......"

I grunted non-commitantly. On my return home that night I discovered quite how arduous his research actually must have been. I sat at my computer, logged onto the Internet and went to the Alta Vista search engine where I typed in the following command `"+Somerset +UK +UFO +Sightings"` and downloaded the information that Garfield had given me earlier in not more than four minutes. However, my mission today was not to start a fight with these two social incompetent wannabes but to try and find out what, if anything, they knew about the air crash, so I figuratively bit my tongue and let him carry on.......

"Because of our position within the UFO community here in Bridgewater, the witness contacted me with his story......"

I interrupted. *"How did he hear of you?"* I asked.

119

"His brother`s a mate of mine" Garfield said *"and....."*

"Tell them about the animal mutilations"..... burst out Tezza, incoherent with excitement that he and his friend were actually involved in a REAL investigation that might even end up in a BOOK!

"Well, yeah" said Garfield, *"we `ad an outbreak of animal mutilation. It `ad to be either Satanists or something to do with UFOs....."*

It turned out, upon questioning, that the `outbreak` was actually two incidents that they`d read about in a local newspaper, both involving puppies. They had not investigated either incident personally, and had merely drawn the conclusion that there was an occult connection with the incidents. One of these incidents was mentioned in a 1999 document issued by Sub-Culture Alternatives Freedom Foundation which places the contemporary legends of animal mutilation into some sensible socio-cultural context, drawing clear parallels with the cases of supposed ritual Satanic Child Abuse a decade before:

"Ironically the history of the Satanic Animal Mutilation Panic provides the clearest evidence yet to DIS-PROVE the doctrine of Ritual Abuse. CHECK THIS OUT: "Cases of Animal Torture and horrible mutilations of animal carcasses have been discovered throughout the U.K. in mysterious situations and bizarre surroundings which point to Satanic ritual Sacrifice. Self-proclaimed experts insist that this is the tip of the iceberg and proof of the existence of an evil pan-global Satanic Conspiracy to debase humanity. As the hysteria builds more cases are being uncovered in YOUR locality! Animal lovers should keep a close watch on anything weird and telephone the RSPCA."

Sound familiar? It should do: Change the words 'animals' to 'children'; swap NSPCC with RSPCA and you have the EXACT same psychological mechanism which foisted the Satanic Child Abuse Hysteria on Britain in 1989. Will the scaremongers succeed again? Fanatics have tried to put the Satanic Animal Mutilation rumour into gear half a dozen times over the past four years. Each time the S.A.F.F. has discredited every claimed case, just like we did with the allegations of Satanic Child Abuse.

During 1990 and 1991 there were over two dozen at-
tempts to float the SAMS scare in Britain. Sensa-
tional headlines like PUPPY IN RITUAL HANGING
(Western Daily Press) or DEVIL RIDDLE OF DEAD FOX IN
CHAPEL (Wales on Sunday). Or how about   SAVE YOUR
PETS - IT'S SATAN'S BIRTHDAY and SATAN LINK FEARS
OVER HORSE INJURIES. Every one of these two dozen
British 'cases' of supposed Satanic Animal Mutilation
was proved to be falsely attributed. Occult connec-
tions were seen where none existed."

Whilst I believe that some animal mutilations do have a fortean significance, the vast majority do not, and indeed, in our increasingly media led
society, stories of animal abuse tug at the heartstrings and are an easy
way to sell newspapers, and unless there is firm and incontrovertible evidence to the contrary they should be ignored because they are often
purely imaginary, or at worst the work of sadistic youths or even children with severe personality disorders who, whilst tragic, have nothing
to do with the main body of fortean research.

However, we seemed to be getting somewhere at last with Garfield and
Tezza, so I did not bother to interrupt them as they rambled on about Satanic Death Cults in Weston Super Mare, but gently brought the subject
back to the air crash in Wellington.

However, not entirely to my surprise, it turned out that the witness in
question was none other than `Badger` whom we had spoken too so
many hours before and that the account that he had given to Garfield and
Tezza was substantially the same as the one that he had given to us. It
took another half hour or so to elicit this information from the terrible
twosome as Tezza kept on interrupting with complete non-sequiturs and
Garfield insisted on holding forth to an annoying degree on every possible aspect of the case.

It turned out in the end that they could tell us nothing that we didn`t al-
ready know, and that all the stuff in `The Blackdown Mystery - The Offi-
cial Report` was just speculation, and ill informed waffle, about greys,
alien bases, and the New World Order. We asked whether there was anyone else around who could tell us anything else about the case, and Garfield said...
"Well, there`s my mate Basil. `E lives with his boyfriend in a hut right in

121

the middle of the levels......"

My heart sunk.

"Is his boyfriend called Danny?"

I asked, already knowing the answer.

"Yeah, cocky little bastard isn`t he?"

We had come full circle.

There being nothing else that we could reasonably get out of either of our two companions we bought them each a beer and left the pub. As we were sitting in the car outside, peering at the map, and trying to work out the best way to get to the Somerset levels, because both Graham and I realised that we would now have to go back to Danny and Basil and see if we could get any sense out of them, there was a knock at the car window. It was Tezza and he obviously had a question of great importance for me

"Er do you know Nick Pope then?" he asked.....

*Proof that not only have I met Nick Pope, but
that I am also taller than he is.
(I`m a better writer as well but that is besides the point)*

CHAPTER EIGHT

The Somerset Levels and Moors lie in the floodplains of eight major rivers or drains, the Kenn, Yeo, Axe, Brue, Huntspill, King's Sedgemoor Drain, Parrett and Tone. The catchment of these rivers is approximately four times the area of the Levels and Moors. At times of high rainfall this can result in large volumes of water moving through the Levels and Moors on their way to the Severn Estuary. The adjacent Natural Areas, therefore, exert a considerable influence on the Somerset Levels and Moors.

The Somerset Levels and Moors Natural Area is essentially formed from a submerged and reclaimed landscape. The geological scenery visible today is of an extensive area of low-lying flat farmland in a basin between the Tickenham Ridge to the north, the Blackdown Hills to the south west, and the Quantock Hills to the west.

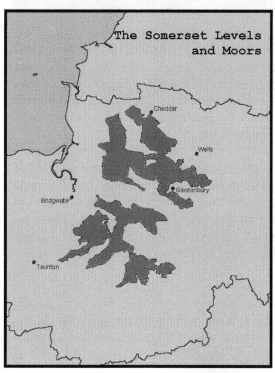

The Somerset Levels and Moors

These land forms have created a special landscape. Dominated by a natural drainage basin, with many areas lying below the level of high tides, the Natural Area has an inherent feeling of wetness. Elevated sea defences and river banks, wide drains and a network of wet rhynes and ditches, together with splashy fields and winter flooding, emphasise the importance of centuries of water control in creating the present landscape from a natural marshland.

The interconnecting network of rivers, drains, rhynes and ditches are the essential arteries of the Somerset Levels and Moors Natural Area. This complex of watercourses has two prime functions - to drain floodwater in winter and to supply water in summer for wet fencing and stock drinking. The balance between these two functions is very fine and current practice has been evolved by several generations of drainage engineers, farmers and, more recently, conservationists.

The levels are a very strange place and it is easy to imagine all sorts of ghosts and ghouls inhabiting the vast expanse of marshes. In the Somerset County Museum in Taunton there are artefacts thousands of years old which were made by the first human inhabitants of the area. These include splatchers - wickerwork `snowshoes` for walking on the soggy marshland very similar to those used by reed and willow farmers to the present day.

The Peat Moors of Somerset lie between the Polden Hills to the south, and the Mendips to the north. The western boundary is the sea in the form of the Bristol Channel, and the city of Wells and the historic town of Glastonbury lie on the eastern limits of the area. This area is known as the Peat Moors, or the "Vale of Avalon" and is characterised by a very flat landscape at, or very near sea level. Until the seventeenth century the whole of this area was flooded during the winter months by the sea, therefore settlements only developed on higher ground, such as Wedmore, Mark and Blackford, to the north, and the settlements on the slopes of the Poldens to the south. Nowadays the sea does not encroach but, despite the extensive network of pumping stations and drainage ditches known as "rhynes" which can be found alongside nearly every road on the moors, winter flooding of fields is still an annual problem.

The levels are dominated, even today, by Glastonbury Tor - a 52 ft high mound that dominates the town of Glastonbury, which is built upon and around its lower slopes. The hill is strongly pyramidal in shape and has upon its green slopes the remnants of a seven-tiered labyrinth, while its summit is crowned with the ruined tower of a fourteenth century church. Many people believe that as Anthony Roberts asserts

"…..they make up part of the Aquarian effigy in that stupendous group of prehistoric monuments known as the Glastonbury Zodiac.

It was this example of ancient technology and magic that Mrs Maltwood found laid out upon the ground in giant forms, revealed only to those minds fired with the spirit of mystical revelation. She published several books on the subject (including an aerial survey) and the true proportions of this beautiful earth sculpture were made graphically apparent. The Glastonbury Zodiac is one of those great 'hidden works' that lies at the roots of all countries' lore and religion, blending physical and metaphysical into a divine coherence.

The form of this terrestrial zodiac, as Mrs Maltwood (and countless later researchers) have uncovered it, is circular with a circumference of thirty miles. Some of the effigies are two or three miles long (eg. Leo, Sagittarius and Pisces) and they are all shaped geomantically from natural features of the land. The effigies are delineated by hills, earthworks, mounds, artificial water courses, old roads, footpaths, streams, and rivers. Notwithstanding this, they all tally with the appropriate star constellations that shine in the sky above them. In other words there was an organically real, natural formation of topographical features forming the basic outlines of the astrological signs which were adapted by shaping through geomancy to make the finished effigies realisable.

Both mystically and physically the earth was moulded to conform to the harmonies of the terrestrial and celestial energy patterns. The grand design is fully apparent only at heights of 20,000 feet and it is obvious that an elevated form of spiritual technology was used to create it. An aerial perspective would have been essential to the logistics of the scheme. The date of this supreme achievement of antiquity is obscure. Some researchers push it as far back as the Atlantean era (10,000 BC) while others, with reference to such works as the Dendarah Zodiac from Egypt, date it to 7000-8000 BC. Mrs Maltwood suggested 2700 BC as a recognition point.

Whatever the date of its initial shaping, the Glastonbury Zodiac set a permanent mystical mark on this area of the British Isles that was the fountainhead for all that followed. The later legends of the Round Table, giants, Arthurian quests for revelation and the secrets of a lost coherence and sanctity, all stem from the memory of this great work carved upon the face of Somerset by men of a forgotten era. They linked earth with heaven in a direct cosmological unity that created the harmony of a now-vanished Golden Age."

Glastonbury also has a strong Christian connection. It is at Glastonbury that legend takes upon itself to go up not only to the beginnings of British Christianity, but also to the beginnings of Christianity itself. The legends of the spot go back to the days of the Apostles. The place is indeed unique, for from the very beginnings of Christianity it was hallowed ground. A legend even tells us that Christ himself as a boy walked upon the hills of Somerset. Such legends are not related to historical facts, but *"the very existence of those legends is a very great fact"*. The immense number of fascinating stories which cling to the place could not have grown up had there not been some substratum of truth behind them. There is, in any case, more than enough of proved history to show that

Glastonbury was for centuries the most ancient and famous centre of Christianity in the land.

For example, the legend of St Joseph of Arimathaea coming to England is of ancient date, and there is also that other lovely tradition that Christ himself in his boyhood came hither. Though improbable it is not impossible, for we know that the Phoenicians came to Britain seeking metals, several centuries before the Christian era. Herodotus, in the fifth century BC, speaks of Cornwall as the Tin Islands, and Greeks too came in search of ore. St Joseph may conceivably have been one of those merchants and have acquired his wealth thus, in which case he might have brought the Holy Child with him on one of his journeys. If he had had this former acquaintance with our island, it would account for Joseph's being chosen as a missionary to Britain by St Philip.

About the middle of the thirteenth century the traditions concerning the coming of St Joseph of Arimathaea to Glastonbury were written down as an introduction to William of Malmesbury's work On the Antiquity of the Church of Glastonbury. We learn from these traditions that the Apostle St Philip sent Joseph of Arimathaea from Gaul with twelve companions to bring the gospel message to our ancestors. This cultivated and wealthy Jew left his home and possessions and all that he had, and now, a poor man, bearing with him the priceless treasures of the true faith and a relic of the Holy Blood, he braved the long and perilous journey which brought him in AD 63 to the shores of Wales and thence travelled across the inland sea [Severn Sea or Bristol Channel] and marshy ground [Somerset Levels] to the Isle of Avalon.

Culturally, however, at least at the very end of the second millenium after Joseph of Arimethea, his heart bursting with the sorrow and pain of witnessing the torture and death of his favourite nephew, finally settled to spend the rest of his life in the tiny settlement in the middle of the Somerset levels, Glastonbury has a different significance. Since the late 1960s it has been a veritable Mecca for successive generations of drug addled hippies determined to tune in to the zeitgeist of Mrs Maltwood, Joseph of Arimethea and a dozen other mystics real and imagined.

In 1970, Michael Eavis, a local farmer and his wife, inspired by the "spirit of the age", held a rock festival on the weekend of September 19th/20th, 1970. It was known then as Pilton Festival, a name it is still sometimes referred to as locally. Michael Eavis was inspired by a visit to the Bath Blues Festival held nearby at Shepton Mallet, where he crawled through a hedge to watch, starting a great Glastonbury tradition. He decided to organise something similar on his land.

As he said several decades later:

"Lots of farmers go to the races, and go hunting and things. But for me, I prefer to do this. It doesn't involve me drinking, for a start, and also I'm at home. I can do it all from the farm."

The Glastonbury Festival of Contemporary Performing Arts, to give it its full title, is a three day festival held most years on a 700 acre site in rural Somerset. The core of the site is Michael Eavis' dairy farm, augmented by land rented from adjoining farms. The entertainment consists of rock and pop on two stages, an acoustic stage, a jazz stage, the Avalon stage, a theatre/cabaret/comedy stage, a cinema tent, dance tent, circus, juggling and just about anything else anybody considers entertaining. The 1970 festival, however, was very different.

"I wanted to pay off my mortgage and farm on a low-key, ecologically sensitive, green-orientated basis." says Eavis with a grin, " Then I would have been a happy man for evermore. In fact, I lost so much money in 1970 that my overdraft got worse."

After The Kinks pulled out, T. Rex were booked as the main attraction, Marc Bolan turning up in a velvet-covered Buick. There were also appearances by *Amazing Blondel, Quintessence, Sam Apple Pie, Steamhammer*, Duster Bennett, Al Stewart, and Keith Christmas, some of whom had only turned up to watch but played anyway. About 2,000 people attended the event, enjoying an ox-roast and free milk from the farm as well as the music. Also in attendance were the local Hell's Angels, who had been inadvertently hired to do security. They set fire to a hay wagon and stole the ox from the roast, but left before causing any Altamont-sized problems.

Many members of swinging London's burgeoning hippy community came down for the weekend, and some of them stayed. Thirty years later, a few of them were still there. One, in particular was Basil.

128

Basil

I'd known Basil for years. In fact, I have a sneaking suspicion that it was me who introduced him to Danny at a drunken Christmas party I had held in the Nurses Home at Langdon Hospital for the Mentally Handi-capped back in the balmy days of 1982.

I had never either liked or disliked him much. He was just this slightly tedious middle aged fat guy with a beatific smile and an untidy mop of curly hair which made him look like a cross between an Old English Sheepdog, a Smurf and the late lamented Gerry Garcia - lead guitarist and founder member of *The Grateful Dead*.

He had wandered in and out of my life for years, talking mystic bollocks but not actually harming anyone. He had always been a little strange. Ru-mour had it that back in 1966 he had been friends with the hip London art gallery crowd which included Peter Blake and Robert Frazer (as well as various members of The Rolling Stones and The Beatles) and as such he had been one of the first people in England to sample the notorious extra-strong LSD made by the American chemist Augustus Owsley and smuggled back to England from the Monterey Festival by various mem-bers of The Beatles inner circle.

Rumour also had it, that Basil took so much of this fabled chemical; the sublime acid of the `Summer of Love` that he tripped out to a place from which he never really returned, and that for the last thirty two years he has been suffering from an amiable drug induced schizophrenia.

I have no idea whether this claim is true, but it certainly fits the facts. Since I've known him, Basil has been what can best be described as a harmless loony. When he inherited a small private income from an eld-erly relative who did everyone (especially Basil) a favour by dying at the age of 93, he was finally freed from the privations of the Social Security system, and left south Devon where he had been living (in comfortable travelling distance of the drop in centre at the local psychiatric hospital) and moved to a small hut, originally built for railwaymen, in the middle of the marshes near to his beloved Glastonbury.

He took Danny with him, and from that day onwards neither of them were seen in what had been their usual haunts. When I met up with Danny again at the Dorchester UFO conference, he had given me some detailed instructions as to how to get to the hut where he and Basil had made their home, and much to my surprise it was relatively easy to find.

After driving around one of the back roads which criss cross the flat expanse of marshes we found the field that contained the little hut in which Danny and Basil had lived for so many years. There was a neat blue Ford Fiesta parked against the bank, and we pulled up behind it.

Entering the field there was no-one to be seen, but through the gathering gloom of a spring dusk we could see Danny and Basil's home on the far side of the field. It was just a hut surrounded by bulrushes. It had no electricity and the only running water was from a semi stagnant drainage ditch about fifteen yards away from what can euphemistically be called their front door. By the time that we arrived dusk was falling. By this time Graham and I had been travelling around Somerset for nearly ten hours and we were both tired and hungry.

"I wonder if your mate Basil will have something for us to eat" speculated Graham hopefully.

"Hmmmmm" I replied. I knew Basil - and Graham did not.

I knocked on the door of the hut hoping that Danny would answer. He was not (and isn't) my favourite person on the planet but at least, most of the time, he talks a fair amount of sense. Unfortunately, it transpired, he wasn't at home, as Basil answered the door.

It was obvious that in the ten years or so since I had seen him last he had deteriorated wildly. He had always been a genial eccentric and ever so slightly mad, but he was hardly recognisable as the wild eyed lunatic who answered the door, and glared at us.

Looking over his shoulders at the interior of the hut I think that even Graham was shocked at the bizarre squalor in which these people existed. Their whole hut was no larger than my sitting room and stank to high heaven. There were badly cured badger skins hanging askew on the walls. A large copper bubble pipe sat in the middle of the floor which was covered in home made rush matting, and there were boxes of books and clothes stashed high against one wall. What I supposed was their bed (actually a broken down mattress covered with sacks and brightly coloured blankets) lay untidily in the other corner and a small but pugnacious bull terrier pup strained at a chain which attached his collar to a staple hammered into one of the end posts of the hut.

"Fuckin` hell," muttered Graham under his breath.....

"Hello Basil, mate," I said with a smile, hoping that he would remember me.

Much to my surprise he did.

"Um `ullo Jon"* he said, evincing no surprise that a bloke he had not seen for a decade should suddenly turn up in a field in the middle of nowhere to talk to him. *"I suppose that you wanted to talk to Danny. Well he doesn`t live here any more........"

He spoke in a quiet, low voice which gave no clue to the emotions he may or may not have been feeling. His voice was more like the purring of a cat than anything that you usually hear from another human being and the whole affect was strangely otherworldly.

"No, Basil, it was you that we wanted to talk to" I said, unsure of whether his statement about his erstwhile lover and shed-mate warranted a response from me or not. *"We`ve been talking to Garfield and Tezza in Bridgewater about the air crash, and we thought that we`d better come and speak to you about it".*

Basil gave no sign that he had understood, or even heard what I had just said, and he turned around and vanished into his hut, emerging again a few minutes later with a half open litre bottle of wine, a lit tilly lamp and a large checked travelling blanket which had seen better days.

He spread the blanket on the ground in front of the hut, placed the tilly lamp on the ground next to him, where it hissed away merrily and he gestured to us to sit down. We sat in silence for a few minutes and took gulps of the rough red wine. The light from the tilly lamp shed an unearthly glow on the dusky landscape and threw strange and alien shadows up on the wall of the hut behind us.

Nightfall in English marshlands in mid April can come almost as fast as it does in the tropics. One minute it is dusk, and the next you can be in almost complete darkness.

It was surprisingly warm. The first grasshoppers of the summer were singing in the reed beds by the river, and we could hear the croaking of a dozen small frogs greeting the late spring night which by now had all but enveloped us in a nurturing shroud. The unrepentant moon and starts tried their best to pierce through the overcast sky but to little avail.

It was a magical moment and none of us seemed willing to break the spell of the marshes at night by talking, so we just sat there in the pale light of the tilly lamp and drank Basil's wine in silence.

Eventually it was Basil who broke the silence. Almost in a whisper he began to recite:

"Now at midnight all the agents
And the superhuman crew
Come out and round up everyone
Who knows more than they do
Then they bring them to the factory
Where the heart-attack machine
Is strapped across their shoulders
And then the kerosene
Is brought down from the castles
By insurance men who go
Check to see that nobody is escaping
To Desolation Row"

I couldn't see Graham's face in the darkness, but I was sure that he wouldn't have recognised the lyric. There didn't seem anything that I could add to it, so I remained silent. The mist began to roll in from the marshes imbuing everything with a damp ethereal spaciness. Basil continued:

"I loved him, you know........and now he's gone."

He was speaking so slowly that each gap between each word seemed like an eternity.

"You mean Danny?"

133

I asked hesitantly.

"Yeah........I`m now completely alone, except at night....THEY come every night"

By this stage, I have to admit that I had absolutely no idea of what he was talking about. I tentatively asked who `They` were, but received more lines of Bob Dylan in reply, all delivered in his low, purring sing-song voice. Then, suddenly his voice changed, and he became once again the University Lecturer he had been before the hallucinogens had permanently robbed him of his reason..

"These marshes are as old as time itself, you know. Nobody knows them like I do anymore and nobody but me knows who and what live here. There are angels and there are daemons and they visit me every night......"

Basil in Extremis

His voice rose to something half way between a whisper and a scream, and he started to quote *Desolation Row* again:

"They're spoon-feeding Casanova
To get him to feel more assured
Then they'll kill him with self-confidence
After poisoning him with words
And the Phantom's shouting to skinny girls
"Get outa here if you don't know"

Graham just sat in the pale glow of the tilly lamp saying nothing as I tried to get some semblance of sense out of this strange middle aged man who had turned his back on everything only to have everything he wanted turn its back on him.

"Tell us about the air crash, Basil" I asked, cajoling him in the voice that one would usually use on a recalcitrant and sickly child.

"he...was...there,...you...know,...he...saw...it....."

Basil started to sob, quietly. He cupped his face in his hands, and rocked backwards and forwards.....

"THEY....did...it...THEY...always...do...it"

his sobbing became more uncontrolled...

"Now the moon is almost hidden
The stars are beginning to hide
The fortune telling lady
Has even taken all her things inside"

He began to snarl as he spat out the next lines:

"All except for Cain and Abel
And the hunchback of Notre Dame
Everybody's making love
Or else expecting rain
And the Good Samaritan, he's dressing
He's getting ready for the show

He's going to the carnival tonight
On Desolation Row"

He hauled himself to his feet and shouted at us:

"Now fuck off and leave me and my family alone, this is private land!"

and he turned off the tilly lamp and left Graham and me in darkness.

CHAPTER NINE

We returned to Exeter in almost complete silence. It had been a peculiar and distressing day, and worse, it had been a day when despite our very best efforts we had achieved practically nothing. `Badger` had told us very little that we had not heard from Danny three weeks before. Sandra and her two friends from BUFOCRAPMRORG had been completely useless, and we had spent the last hours of our investigation sitting in a marshy field listening to a middle aged acid casualty quoting Bob Dylan.

I was convinced (or to be more honest, I had managed to convince myself that I was convinced) that Basil had experienced something traumatic which had evinced the reactions that we had seen the previous night. After all, as I told Graham, desperately trying to convince both him and me that there was still a case here worth investigating, I had known Basil intermittently for years and whilst he had always been somewhat vacant, OK, not to put too fine a point on it the guy had always been a complete loony, but he had not been like this. I had never known him ramble or scream, and I had never seen him get even verbally violent before.

Who were these marsh daemons who visited him every night? He lived alone, now Danny had gone, so who were `his family` that he wanted us to leave alone? He kept on saying that `They` had caused the air crash, but who were `They`?

Was something genuinely sinister at work here? Or were these just the ravings of drug induced schizophrenia? I desperately wanted it to be the former, but like Graham I strongly suspected that the latter scenario was the truth.

The most important question which faced us was what on earth were we going to do next? Everywhere we had looked the investigation had drawn a blank and it strongly seemed as if there were no more avenues that we could explore.

We got home, drank a cup of tea and retired to our respective rooms to sleep.

The next morning at about half past eleven we were awoken rudely by the arrival of The World`s only Gothic Cryptozoologist [TM], who, told us of his adventures in the punk club with Nick Redfern and his singular failure to have sex with the heroin addled prostitute called Our Nina.

As I sit here typing this story, a month or so after the events in this book, and, indeed, a month after we eventually managed to solve the case to everyone`s satisfaction, it is half past four in the morning and the dawn is breaking across the Exeter skyline. Reading back over what I have written about me, and more importantly about Graham and Richard, I feel that it could be argued that I have shown all three of us up in a fairly unfavourable light. Yes, Richard is an arrogant weirdo who visits prostitutes, Graham and I border on the psychopathic, and have often been known to drink too much, my sojourns in psychotherapy have been recounted elsewhere, and all three of us have a curious aversion towards what might be described as normal employment. It could well be argued that I have portrayed the three of us as dissolute sociopaths, and indeed it could equally well be argued that this is exactly what we are.

However, it is precisely because of these flaws in our characters that we are able to do what we do so well. We live and work on the fringes of society and the fringes of science and our job is to chronicle and explore events that are outside of and alien to the belief systems of most people. It is precisely because of the nature of what we do that sometimes our behaviour is more extreme that that of many people within society.

Another factor is that it so happens that at the time that the events in this story were unfolding around us all three of us were single. The previous year all three of us had been in relationships, and no doubt all three of us would be again, but during the spring and early summer of 1999 all three of us were living a bachelor lifestyle with the attendant excesses thereof....and enjoying every minute of it.

Over a few drinks that lunchtime we compared notes. From what Richard told us that he had gleaned from Nick Redfern there was no doubt that there had been incidents before which involved RAF `planes and unidentified flying objects, and despite the lamentable lack of solid evidence it did appear that something strange had happened the night a RAF Harrier had crashed into the wild Blackdown Hills. We had a case, but we were a long way from solving it, and for the moment we had far more pressing matters to attend to.

There were only three more days to go until the annual *Fortean Times* Unconvention. Billed as `A weekend of the weird` this weekend is in many ways the high spot of our year. It is not only a chance for us to meet fellow travellers along the less charted byways of fringe science, forteans and general strangeness but is usually the financial highlight of our year as far as selling our wares, and gaining new subscribers to the two magazines that we publish.

In many ways it also acts for us in the same way as a nineteenth century `Hiring fair` did for artisans and workmen of previous generations. It is the best chance we get all year to meet TV producers and magazine editors and get a modicum of respectable employment to help us through the following twelve months. All three of us had lectured at previous Unconventions and although none of us were scheduled to appear at the 1999 event we were all looking forward to it immensely.

We had to put our investigations into the Blackdown Mystery on the figurative back burner for a while therefore as we dedicated all of our efforts towards making sure that we had a profitable and enjoyable weekend. As already chronicled, however, it is a great pity that none of us thought to make a thorough check of the tyres and wheel tracking of our poor beleaguered Nissan Bluebird.

On the morning of the 24th, by the time that we had finished dealing with the police we were running an hour and a half behind schedule. We had been fortunate enough to persuade the forces of law and order not to impound the car and to allow us to continue to our destination on the strict proviso that we had the defective tyres replaced immediately. Luckily we had unloaded our wares the night before and we had already set up our stall so, dropping Richard outside the Commonwealth Institute in Kensington High Street with strict instructions to make as much money as was humanly possible, Graham and I drove on towards Wood Lane where we found a tyre depot to make our vehicle legal again.

While Graham stayed with the car I walked around the corner and found the nearest National Westminster cash machine and drew out the last £150 of my overdraft with which to pay for the new tyres. When, an hour or so later, we had done so, I was left with the stunning sum of £8.50 left in all the world to survive on. Graham telephoned the number we had been given by the police to confirm that we had changed our tyres and was told that before we could drive the car anywhere we had to have it inspected by the same policemen who had stopped us earlier that morning in order to confirm that the vehicle was now in a roadworthy state.

It was now nearly noon, and I was getting more and more concerned about what might be happening back at the Unconvention in my absence. Richard had never been left alone for any length of time on one of our stalls before, and therefore his sales technique (especially as regards second hand books on subjects like UFOs about which he knew nothing and cared less) was an unproven commodity. I therefore left Graham to wait for the police and invested the greater part of my remaining funds in a taxi to take me back to the convention venue.

The Commercial Wing of the CFZ

I needn't have worried as things transpired. Richard had been doing a roaring trade and had already made a respectable sum of money. The sight of a healthy bundle of ten pound notes in a cardboard box behind

the stall lifted my spirits somewhat and I began to relax and set my mind towards the real business of the weekend.

Sharing a stall with the CFZ posse was my publisher at the time. I greeted them warmly and was rewarded with a hail of invective from my publisher who told me that I was a complete bloody fool to have even thought of driving one of my dodgy motors through Whitehall in the middle of a serious security alert. It was the first that I had heard of any security problems, and it was only then that I realised quite how stupid, and indeed foolhardy, we had been.

Never mind, I thought, at least we were making money, but then the horrible truth hit me. Despite the fact that I had just paid out £141.50 on getting four new tyres I would still have to get a new MoT certificate upon our return to Exeter or else buy a new car. Either option was likely to cost a severe amount of money, and upon doing sum quick sums in my head I realised that we were going to have to make an unprecedented takings over the next two days in order to break even let alone make a profit and that far from everything being alright we were actually in deep trouble.

Just then, Graham arrived looking serious. he confirmed what I had just realised, and told me that furthermore he had been talking to a friendly fellow at the garage in Wood Lane who estimated that it was going to be completely uneconomic to put the Nissan through a MoT test and that we were certainly going to have to buy a new car.

At this point I was practically in tears and I had absolutely no idea what I was going to do next. My cash flow situation has always been precarious. It is one of the undeniable aspects of being both self employed and working in an area as abstract as practical forteana that ones earnings are few and far between. I needed a miracle or preferably a visit from my fairy godfather in order to avoid looming bankruptcy.

Was there a connection between this incident and the one which Danny had told us about? My initial reaction was `No` but we had to find out. The United Kingdom Air Accidents Investigation Branch (AAIB)

Then, suddenly, with a flash of gossamer wings (OK, I exaggerate a bit) my fairy godfather appeared on the scene in the shape of my then pub-

lisher. *"Why don't you do another book for me Jon?"* he said, *"then I can give you an advance and you can buy a new car and pay the driving fine on the old one".*

I nearly hugged him. This was a gift from the Gods. But I knew that he was still smarting over my failure to provide a book on the other UFO case that I have alluded to earler—the one that was even more complete bollocks than this one. However, what did he want me to write a book about?

"Well, what are you working on at the moment?"

Suddenly the world seemed black again and I fell back into a slough of despondency as I explained that although we were currently investigating what we had come to call the Blackdown Mystery, all the witnesses that we had dealt with were either social undesirables or barking mad and that it seemed unlikely that we were going to be able to reach a firm conclusion.

My publisher laughed. *"The trouble with all of your other books, Jon, is that you make your investigations seem too bloody easy. Why not tell it like it is? Stop pretending to be some kind of fortean superman and explain the sheer frustration and general nitty gritty of a real investigation? That would make a REALLY good book".*

I winced and asked him whether he wouldn't prefer a slightly sanitised version of events. Surely, I insisted, people didn't want to read about middle aged schizophrenics quoting Bob Dylan in muddy fields while Richard chased prostitutes around the seamier parts of the Black Country.....

"Wrong" he said. "As long as there is actually a mystery to solve, that is exactly what people would like to read".

"Bloody hell" I grunted disbelievingly. *"Well, if you're sure"......*

and we shook hands. A deal had been done.

However, although my immediate financial predicament had been solved I was faced with a new dilemma. Whereas until now the search for the

truth behind the Blackdown Mystery had been an intellectual pursuit, now we had been forced into the position where we had to find out the facts behind the case, and I, for one, still had no idea whatsoever how we were going to do this.

During the rest of that weekend, whilst Richard and Graham did their best to sell things, I desperately ran around every UFOlogist that I knew at the convention asking them all whether they had heard anything at all about the case. Not really to my surprise none of them had and I was beginning to panic. If no-one could give me any firm facts how the hell was I going to either solve the case or be able to write a book about it? This was getting serious.

The rest of the weekend passed relatively unexceptionally and we returned to Exeter on the Monday night. Although it was imperative that we get on with our investigation there were other things that merited our attention and we were not to carry on our hunt for the truth to any great degree until the following weekend.

Tuesday and Wednesday were spent trying to buy a new car. Whereas I had always planned to scrap the Nissan when the MoT ran out, I had assumed that I was going to have more money at my disposal than was actually the case, and it has to be said that trying to buy a half decent vehicle during 1999 when you only have a budget of four hundred pounds is easier said than done.

It actually took us two whole days to find the car we eventually bought. We looked at five cars on the Tuesday - each of them more decrepit and worn out than the last. I think that the nadir of our experience was the Vauxhall Carlton with three bald tyres, no exhaust and which belched steam out of the radiator when the engine had been running for more than five minutes. We were unwilling to accept the explanation of the owner that it was just a little cranky after having been left unused for six weeks, and on the Tuesday night we returned to CFZ Mansions even more disconsolate than we had been in the immediate aftermath of our run in with the Metropolitan Police.

By this time of course, the Nissan was totally illegal and we were taking a dreadful risk each time that we took her out onto the open road. Much to our great joy, however, half way through Wednesday afternoon we found a large and opulent looking Rover which was just within our price range and which furthermore had nearly twelve months MoT and several months of tax. Graham and I looked at each other with relief and immediately handed over a grubby bundle of ten pound notes. At least one problem was solved for the time being!

The next day was a particularly sad one. Our next door neighbour - a lady of whom we had all grown particularly fond - had died and we had to attend her funeral, at which I read the eulogy. After the funeral none of us felt able to do any work, and so all three of us retired to our rooms to be alone with our thoughts and our memories.

Friday the 30th April dawned bright and clear, but once again we were unable to make any progress with the Blackdown Mystery. It was Bealtaine.
The name of the fertility festival of Bealtaine means "good fire", and bonfires were once used to mark the symbolic return of the Summer sun and renewed life. The Celts have a God named Bel, meaning "Lord", who is known as "The Bright One" - a God of light and fire. Bealtaine celebrates the return of the light and its life-giving force upon the Earth.

Bealtaine is a powerful holiday, filled with legend and tradition that goes back farther than most recorded history. One of the most famous is probably the Maypole, a tall pole of oak adorned with a hawthorne garland and many brightly coloured ribbons. The ribbons would be held by the many participants who danced their way around the Maypole in opposing directions, weaving in and out until the people were almost arm in arm and the Maypole was woven with bright springtime colours from top to bottom. The Maypole is actually a symbol for fertility of the land, and the ribbons being wound represent the movement of energies between the Earth and the Sky (The Goddess and the God) that causes the plants to grow and the world to re-awaken.

Besides being a celebration of the fertility of the earth and the renewed growth of crops, what we must realise is that the cycle of planting and growth does not only pertain to physical plants, but also to our spirituality as a whole. Bealtaine should be a time to plant the seeds of spiritual growth and development in us all, praising the God and Goddess for the great gifts they have given us all.

I am a Christian, not a Pagan, but many of my friends (including Richard) are devotees of the old religion and I have always been particularly interested in the rituals of Celtic Paganism. Months before, the Exeter Strange Phenomena Group, which Graham and I had founded in the autumn of 1996 had agreed to stage a Bealtaine ritual in Manna Woods near Falmouth in Cornwall with the intention of attempting to invoke the grotesque Owlman which has been reported in these woods for over twenty years.

In my 1997 book *The Owlman and Others* I describe my five year quest for the truth surrounding this grotesque zooform apparition. One of the early witnesses described it in graphic detail:

"It has red slanting eyes and a very large mouth. The feathers are silvery grey and so are his body and legs, the feet are like a big, black, crab's claws. We were frightened at the time. It was so strange, like something ut of a horror film. After the thing went up, there were crackling sounds in the tree-tops for ages. Our mother thinks we made it all up just because we read about these things, but that is not true. we really saw the bird-man, though it could have been someone playing a trick in a very good costume and make up. But how could it rise up like that? If we imagined it, then we both imagined it at the same time".

In 1978, 1980 and 1986, the infamous Irish wizard Tony `Doc` Shiels had carried out magickal rituals either at Bealtaine or Samhain (Hallow`een) to invoke `His Owliness` and partly as an intellectual discipline and partly out of sheer mischievous caprice we decided to emulate him on then last Walpurgis Night of the 20th Century.

Various members of the Exeter Strange Phenomena Group decided to come along for the ride, and we were also accompanied by veteran Australian cryptozoologist Tony Healy co-author of a remarkable book called Out of the Shadows. Tony had arrived in Exeter that afternoon. We had met him at the Unconvention, and as is our custom we had invited him to stay with us for as long as he wanted.

One of the less well publicised roles of the Centre for Fortean Zoology is that it acts as a flop house for visiting forteans from around the world and at various times one can find several well known members of the fortean and cryptoinvestigative communities wrapped in blankets or sleeping bags on my sitting room floor.

Tony was not the only minor celebrity to accompany us on our magickal quest. One of the party was a long haired and bearded young man wearing a ragged Medieval Court Jester's outfit. Perhaps appropriately, he answered to the name of `Jester`.

In 1994 sixty-five miles of improvement work began on the A30 and the A35 between Exeter, Devon and Bere Regis, Dorset. The road was let to an Anglo-German road building consortium called, "Connect", under a "Design, Build, Finance, Operate" (DBFO) project. The consortium who financed and built the road, is to be paid by the government in the form of "shadow tolls". These tolls involve the final bill for the tax payer, depending upon the amount of traffic using the new road. The thirteen mile by-pass between Honiton and Exeter, is part of this road improvement work, and is estimated to cost around sixty-five million pounds.

Three small protests camps were set up along this part of the road construction work. The two protest camps at Allercombe and Trollheim, were cleared by the authorities on the 27th December 1996, and 12th January 1997 respectively. However, the protest camp at Fairmile still remained.

The camp at Fairmile was unique. Not only did it contain the usual tree houses, or "twigloos", but it also had an elaborate network of underground tunnels. Five protesters barricaded themselves in these tunnels, behind steel and wooden doors in excavations of thirty to forty feet deep. Matters for removing the protesters from the tunnels were heightened by the unstable sandy soil. In order to stop any other protesters joining those in the tunnels, the two hundred and fifty security guards and police erected a triple barrier; a six foot wooden fence, razor wire and a ten foot steel fence. The authorities used ground radar in order to survey the tunnel network, and tunnelling experts were linked by video cameras to their colleagues on the surface.

The last tunnelling protester, Daniel Needs, or "Swampy" as he is known, emerged from the tunnels on Friday, January 31st, after spending six nights underground. He explained: *"I stopped digging because I felt we had made our point and by coming out it was safer for all concerned"*. He said he would be prepared to do the same again, even if it

Invocation of his daemon brother

147

meant arrest. He told television and newspaper reporters: *"It is the only way to get a voice these days. If I wrote a letter to my M.P., would I have achieved all this? Would you lot be here now?"*.

Whilst Swampy achieved a modicum of national fame as a result of his road protesting activities, most of the people involved in the road protest camp remained relatively obscure. One of the few members of this itinerant though well meaning community to reach a level of notoriety in the national press was `Jester`. Clad in his eponymous costume he had spent the months leading up to the evictions as a merry maker and a jester whose role was to keep the spirits of the beleaguered protesters uplifted and to bait the oncoming forces of law, order and destruction. As a result of his activities he was charged with several public order offences but that, like so much hinted at in this book is undoubtedly another story!

When the road protest finally finished `Jester` hung up his cap and bells and returned to his studies of folklore and the occult and, more by luck than by judgement ended up at one of the meetings of the Exeter Strange Phenomena Group in early 1999, where he soon became a fixture.

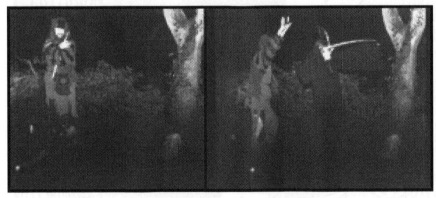

Jester and Richard do their thing

(Pix © Tony Healey)

He had read my book about the Owlman and was determined to help us in any way during our attempts to invoke the beastie. Together with Richard (in the guise of `Muzzlehutch the Magician`) he performed a theatrical and exciting ritual in the woods below Mawnan Old Church to the rapturous applause of the rest of use who looked on in awe.

This is not the time nor the place to describe the ritual in any detail. No doubt, I shall do that elsewhere. What is important as far as this particular narrative is concerned is what happened in the pub in the village of Mawnan Smith immediately after the ritual.

Invocation in Mawnan Woods

(Pix © Tony Healey)

The eight of us who had participated in, filmed and watched the Bealtaine ritual were sitting in a quiet corner of the saloon bar of the *Old Red Lion,* sipping beer and desultorily discussing the arcane business of the Exeter Strange Phenomena Group, when somebody (I think it was Richard) brought up the subject of The Blackdown Mystery.

Many of the group hadn`t heard anything about it, so pressed for details I explained the details of our quest. How Danny had told us about the mystery originally and how when we had managed to track down the elusive `Badger` he had told us much the same story, but that the only corroborative evidence that he had been able to give us that he had actually been in the place that he claimed to have been at the time that the event happened was the word of an escaped prisoner with an anthropomorphic nickname.

*"Erm, he wasn`t called `Ratty` by any chance was he?"* piped up `Jester` from the corner of the bar.

"Yes he was" I said in an incredibly surprised voice. *"How the hell did you know?"*

"I`ve got some documents at home that I think you might find interesting" chuckled Jester *"I`ll bring them over on Tuesday"* and refusing to say anything more he changed the subject and sat at his end of the table looking inscrutable.

CHAPTER TEN

Jester had insisted that we leave him in Cornwall on the Friday night as he wanted to spend some time alone in the woods in the hope that the owlman would manifest himself before him.

This we did and we spent much of the weekend getting drunk with Tony and making plans for the next week. Monday was a Bank Holiday and thus there was nothing we could do until the following day.

On the Tuesday morning Graham tried again to contact the elusive Wing Commander X. When he finally got through to the RAF Inspectorate of Crashes he was told in no uncertain terms that there had been NO crash of any RAF aircraft in the Blackdown Hills during 1995 and that there was nothing further that Wing Commander X or his colleagues would be able to do for us.

Concluding this conversation, Graham, for the first time began to accept that something fishy might well be going on. We knew that there had been a crash. Why the hell wouldn`t anyone in authority admit it?

Our incipient paranoia was fuelled immensely by the mood in the country at the time. ABC News on the 1st May reported:

"What was first thought to require only a few days of bombing may soon result in a deadly ground war and a peacekeeping mission lasting years. The deluge of ethnic Albanian refugees and the daunting challenge of safely returning them to Kosovo reflects a present failure more than signs of impending success. Critics blame NATO itself for a lack of success in the war, made worse by the messy business of forging consensus among 19 members for decisive action on the battlefield. Even after voting on a limited air war against Yugoslavia, several members differed over the scale of the offensive and what targets to strike. "I have never been more fearful for NATO's future," Sen. Gordon Smith, R-Ore., chairman of the Senate Subcommittee on European Affairs, said this week. "I fear, if the present trend continues in the war with Yugoslavia, that a belief will arise in Congress and among the American people that but for NATO, we would not be in this fight and because of NATO, we can't win."

In pubs across the land people spent the Bank Holiday weekend speculating that what had originally been a minor police action was going to escalate into all out war, and that it seemed ever more likely that the Russians, who had been expressing their strong disapproval of the NATO action would be drawn into a wider conflict. For the first time in a decade and a half people were beginning to think in terms of the possibility that a third world war might be imminent.

Against this background the blank wall of silence that we had encountered from the RAF began to assume ever more sinister proportions and we began to think that perhaps we had bitten off far more than we could easily chew.

On a practical level we had once again run into a figurative stone wall, and we had no real idea how our investigation could proceed any further. Richard had to return an overdue library book so he volunteered to go back to Exeter library and carry out one last search through the newspapers there for any reports of the crash. We agreed that if he wasn't able to come up with anything this time that, at least for the time being the case would have to rest. We had spent far too much time on it already, and I was beginning to mentally prepare myself for telling my publisher that I wasn't going to be able to write this book and that I would have to return the advance.

Once again I was facing the threat of what seemed like imminent bankruptcy and I had absolutely no idea what to do about it.

Richard was at the library, Graham was playing *Doom* and I was sitting on the sofa listening to Scott Walker and quietly panicking, when there was a knock on the door. It was `Jester`, clutching a sheaf of papers and grinning so widely that it looked as if his face was going to split in two.

He continued to grin, and silently passed me the papers which were to be the breakthrough in our investigation. I was just about to look at them when the telephone rang. It was Richard.

"I've solved the bloody mystery! I know WHY the RAF denied all knowl-

edge and WHY you couldn`t find any details of the crash in the November newspapers"

he shouted down the telephone in delight, but refused to give any more details.

"You`ll know soon enough"* he laughed, *"I`ll be back as quickly as I can"

The documents that `Jester` passed to me turned out to be two police statements by `Ratty` whose real name turned out to be Nicholas Pointer. I will quote the first page of one document:

STATEMENT: Nicholas Pointer of H.M. Prison, Exeter will say as follows:

I am born Nicholas Pointer and I am currently a serving prisoner at H.M.Prison, Exeter. I was born on the 15th June 1953 and I am therefore currently aged 44 years. I am charged with four offences on the same Indictment. I intend to plead as follows:-

1.   Causing grievous bodily harm to John McArdle on the 13th May 1997 - I indent [sic] to plead not guilty Attempted robbery of John McArdle on the same day - I intend to plead not guilty.

2.   Theft of a Subaru motor car between the 12th May 1997 and the 15th May 1997 -I intend to plead guilty.

3.   Taking a conveyance without authority between the 24th January 1997 and the 27th January 1997 - I intend to plead guilty.

I am due to appear before Exeter Crown Court for plea and directions hearing on the 22nd August 1997 at 10.30. a.m. I am currently serving a life sentence of imprisonment imposed in 1974. This was for an offence of murder.

The brief circumstances of the original offence are that at the time of the offence, I was on the run from Borstal. I had no accommodation, was cold and hungry. I came across what appeared to be an empty

flat and broke in with a view to finding clothes and food to eat. During the course of the break-in, I was disturbed by the householder. I had found a metal pipe which I was using to try and force a drawer open. Unfortunately, at the time I was disturbed, I had that pipe in my hand and when disturbed, turned around and hit out with it. Unfortunately, I struck the householder with the pipe with the result that he died.

I duly appeared before the Crown Court in 1973 where I pleaded guilty to a charge of murder and received a life sentence of imprisonment.

Because the second document which, although it makes no mention of UFOs, is not only fascinating. but proved to be germane to our finding out the definitive truth behind the reality of `Badgers` testimony I make no apologies for having quoted pretty well in full.

FROM 1700381 POINTER H M PRISON EXETER
2 September 1997

I have been asked to write down everything that I have done since I absconded from HMP Sudbury on 17 July 1996. 1 will try to remember as much as I can. I suppose I should begin by giving my reasons for the abscond. During my time in Sudbury last year I was given a statutory urine test which proved positive. I was informed by the Governor that if I was either found to have used cannabis on the next test or placed on report for any other offence whilst in his prison, I could expect to be returned to closed conditions, which as you are no doubt aware, would in my situation at that time, have resulted in at least another 4-6 years in prison. I have to say that I don't think I would have been able to do those extra years without losing a great deal of the strength of mind that I have gained up until then. I did however attempt to conform to the Rules in Sudbury. And until the night of my abscond, I had stayed off of drugs and other substances which would have cost me the extra years.

On the night of the 1 6th July, 1 was in my room,

listening to some music, I'm not sure at what time I received a knock at my door, but it must have been after midnight. When I opened the door I saw an ex-inmate friend of mine who had crept into the Prison to bring me a parcel of Tobacco, Cannabis and a bottle of Scotch. He also had with him a pair of women friends. I could at that time have, in all probability, been able to refuse the Cannabis and Drink but there was no way I could have said No to spending some time making love to a good looking woman. Rather than take the chance on being caught by the night staff on patrol in the prison, the four of us went into the woods beside the prison where we had a drink or two and I and the lass in question let nature take its course. There was NO intent on my part to abscond, I couldn't afford to screw up anymore with the Home Office.

About 4 o'clock the other two [my pal and his girl] noticed a lot of activity inside the prison and realised that I had been found to be missing. I knew that I'd had it. There was no way I could get back into my room without being caught and realised that I was in the shit and in danger of drowning in it. Even then I would probably have returned but when Sarah, the girl I was with, offered me a way to run [my biggest weakness - running away from problems] I grabbed it with both hands.

I was able to get a lift from them all the way to Worcester where they dropped me off. During the next few days l hitched and walked into Devon where I met the A30 Road Protesters and lived on the Fairmile site. I left Fairmile for a while to go to Sidmouth for the International Folk Festival. By then I had reasoned that the only real chance I had to minimise the penalty and punishment I would receive eventually was to "not break the Law". I stole nothing from anyone whilst in Sidmouth and left there with a growing belief that I could prove not only to the Home Office, but in some ways, more importantly, to myself, that I was able to live outside of Prison without getting into trouble. From the end of the Sidmouth Festival until the last week of September l spent my time either on the Fairmile/Trollheim sites or staying with a couple that I had met at the Festival; during that time I earned a few £5 a week [sic] doing odd jobs on the farms in the Southleigh - Ottery St Mary - Honiton area mostly agricultural labouring etc. I didn't steal.

At the end of September I was staying in a Bender [traveller's canvas hut] in woods near Southleigh when numerous armed Police, Helicopters, dogs, etc. arrested me at about 10.00 on a Tuesday night. I was convinced that they knew who I was and that this was it". When I discovered that they had no idea of my true identity I lied my head off and freely admit it. I gave my name as Kevin NEWELL and explained that I was an old style traveller, no record, no involvement with the Law at all except the odd warning for Poaching and Trespass. I was taken to Axminster Police Station, questioned and then moved to Exeter Police Station where I was questioned again. Eventually I was charged with Trespass with a Firearm [a 22 air rifle] and the theft of a "Skip Lamp". I was cautioned and released. The air rifle was returned and after I agreed to return to the A30 sites and pass on information to the Devon/Cornwall Police about the tunnels under the sites I was given a lift back to Southleigh, so that I could collect the rest of my belongings from the Bender in the Woods. I signed a receipt for £ 10 [phone expenses for my tunnel info] and the Police Officers left. I went back to Fairmile. At that time I was starting to believe that by living a legal life, Karma was turning my way. Not only didn't I end up back in prison, but the Police didn't even bother to look for me again even though I was staying at Fairmile and phoning in each Tuesday for about 5 weeks. I was aware that the Police had to know who I was after they had sent my finger prints etc in to the CR0 computer and would probably arrest me at any time. I didn't allow myself to run away. [By now I was determined not to let fear drive me into a deeper hole than the one I was already in]. When I did leave the A30 protest I had established myself as the "Pixie King" organising the alarms and other early warning systems to let us know when the "Sheriff and his men in Black" were coming. I didn't hide. From Fairmile I travelled to Dartmoor for the

Samhain gathering in Merryvale which was a gathering of the Tvatha De Danaan, the Children of the Earth Mother. [I have been involved in Her way for many years now and during my recent abscond, I had the honour to become one of Her "priests"].

From Merryvale I spent some time with the Donga tribe and was with them during the eviction from Dartmoor at the beginning of November. Still I was-n't stealing or becoming aggressive either physi-cally or verbally. I must admit to becoming a little bit complacent, even approaching the officers who were videoing the eviction and bantering with them.

I left the Dongas a few days later and returned to Fairmile and eventually Southleigh where my arrival started the tongues wagging to say the least. My ar-rest etc the previous September had made me and my face very recognisable. This was probably 4-5 weeks before Christmas.

While I was staying in Southleigh I was earning my money by working as a beater on the Gittisham Estate as well as by selling Rabbits, Pheasants and Trout, that I admit to Poaching. Most of the locals had the game [sic] from me at one time or another. Country folk don't see buying a poached Trout as being that much of a crime, especially when its not only very fresh, but also a damn site cheaper than from the shop.

I stayed in Southleigh until the beginning of Janu-ary when I left to visit friends in Wales. I didn't want to go at the time mainly because the weather was very cold and hitching with backpack, tent etc. is an almost certain way to draw the attention of any bored policeman. The overriding cause of my leaving was the guy whose place I had been staying

---

AUTHOR'S NOTE: This document is 100% real, and has not been edited in any way. The one thing that I find amazing is that Senor Ratty actually believed that spouting a load of hippy bollocks was going to help his case!

at. Nik is not the most stable of guys, and when I was daft enough to be a bit too obvious where my feelings for Charlotte [his girlfriend] were concerned he flipped. I freely admit to taking their Ford Escort estate and driving it to Malvern [where I left it]. I can handle the ordinary physical threats without too much trouble, but having an automatic pistol waved in my face and being told that if I ever looked at Charlotte again he'd "blow my balls off" wasn't in the same ball park. I got the hell out of Devon as quickly as I could. I pinched the car. [It was the first thing I had stolen since I absconded in July - unless Pheasant and Rabbit etc fall into the same]. I've never been able to see how any Bird, Animal or Fish can belong to anyone. The Mother gave all of us our life and would receive us all back again

His next words made me suspect the second explanation for his motives.

[Man and Animal, Fish and Fowl, we are all free in Her eyes]. Sorry, I am losing the path. I admit I stole the car, but only to leave as quickly as I could. After leaving the motor I hitched my way back into Gloucester where I spent the next months until my arrest on the 15th May this year. On the 3rd of February I went to the local Job Centre and knew that [sic], but I still believed that I could be "Legal". When to the staff in the Job Centre [sic] that my original family name father had changed it to PATTERSON when I was a babe. [Y52 1361 9B] and DOB. Half expecting the police to arrive didn't happen. "signed on" - it was a risk I went to sign on I explained was POINTER but that my I gave my correct NI No. to arrest me on the spot, it During the time I was living in Gloucester I came to the attention of the Police twice. The first time was when I was asked to see someone in the Drug Squad. I eventually saw two DS officers and informed them that there were some very nasty guys doing large deals in hard drugs using the Cafe opposite the Night Shelter. I admit that the only reason I did this was for my woman friend who was staying in the B & B above the Cafe, she had only just been released from Wootton Lawn Psychiatric Hospital in Gloucester and had been lucky to survive a bad Heroin habit. I didn't want her to fall backwards into the hard drug scene and I know how easy that can be when its right under your nose. The DS Officers know me as Nicholas PATTERSON, they also know what I was prepared to grass people up.

The only other occasion that I am aware of when the Police looked my way was when I had an altercation with a guy outside the Shelter one night, also because of Heroin. He had apparently been spreading rumours that Karen was back on Heroin. It was his way of trying to get at a friend of mine who was also involved with Karen, he was supposed to have given her a fix and given her some crack! It almost worked, I have to confess that when I first heard that he had given her some "H" I wanted to knock seven bales out of him, I went as far as confronting him and her at the Night Shelter. I know enough about the effects of Heroin and about lying to realise that the story was a load of crap. The source of the rumour turned out to be another guy who felt that he had found a way to give my mate Gary some grief for his own twisted reasons. The Police came into it when I thumped him outside the Shelter and he went to the law. They rang the staff on duty that evening in the shelter to find out what was going on. I believe the staff member was a guy called ANDY. They were told why he was thumped and after I gave my word not to carry on with things they left it. I made many good friends over my time in and around Gloucester, most of them female [I admit to being arrogant when it comes to women, I love em and know that I can be the Toad]. I had been spending a lot of time outside of Gloucester in Candleford where I was seeing two girls most weekends. Samantha who is now 20 was the daughter of a volunteer in the Shelter and managed to get her mother and father to accept me spending weekends with her and her 19 year old friend in their flat. I am only mentioning this to illustrate how little aggression or threat people find in me. At the end of April I signed off of the Dole because I had been offered a job in the Forest of Dean on the Rainbow 2,000 site. I signed off so that I couldn't be done for fraud. On Monday 12th May I thumbed down to Devon to see some of the Fairmile Pixies to find out if they were going to go to Manchester. After a very heavy party I stole

a Subaru Pick-up from Southleigh and drove back to
Gloucester. I was arrested on the Wednesday evening
about 8.15. From there I have been told that I am being charged with Attempted Murder and Robbery for a
set of keys. To be blunt "Bollocks". I am prepared to
answer that in open court and am confident that I
will win.
I am prepared to be punished for my actions, but I
will NOT pay for something I haven't done.

                SIGNED   N POINTER

It was clear from these documents that `Badger` had to have been lying.
If Nicholas Pointer had not escaped from HMP Sudbury until the seventeenth of July 1996 then he could *not* have been in the Blackdown Hills
with `Badger` in November 1995, and if `Badger` had been lying about
something as fundamental as this then it placed the veracity of the rest of
his account in serious jeopardy.

Just then Richard burst through the door and thrust a photocopied newspaper article into my hand. It was dated Saturday, February 24th 1996
and was from *The Western Morning News*. It read:

A ROYAL Navy Sea Harrier jump jet crashed yesterday
on a training exercise over Somerset killing its two
crew. The £14 million Sea Harrier T4 training aircraft was on exercise from RNAS Yeovilton when it
plunged into the field on the Blackdown Hills just
after 2.30pm. The aircraft crossed a country road
near the *Merry Harriers* Pub, near Burnworthy, and
ripped through trees into a field, with some wreckage
ending up on the edge of a pond. The two man crew
died instantly as the aircraft broke up on Impact and
wreckage was strewn over 300 yards. There were no
other casualties and the two victims are not being
named until their families have been informed. Police
closed roads around the site of the crash which is
about four miles south east of Wellington. One of the
first eyewitnesses on the scene told how he came
across the remains of the Harrier burning in a copse
300 yards from the road he was driving along.

Local carpenter Stephen Holway said: *"We thought the
pilot might have ejected or something so ran across*

the field towards the wreck." Mr Holway, 28, from Wellington, said the plane had narrowly missed ploughing into a house by the side of the road. "One of the men who ran out to help said it had passed right over his head and had just missed his house," he said. Debris from the crash was spread out over 500 yards, he said and he believed the plane must have ploughed through banks of trees and hedges before skipping over the road and crash-landing in the copse.

"The hedges on both sides of the road were on fire. They had been wiped out for 200 yards. There were bits of metal everywhere and what looked like the turbine from the engine lying in the road," he said.

John Floyde, 66, who lives in a cottage a quarter of a mile from the crash scene, said the impact shook his cottage on the .Burnworthy Estate, and rattled the windows. "I stood on a gate and saw bits of wreckage in a field right beside the road," he said. Mr Floyde said because people who lived in the area were so near the Yeovilton air base they did not take much notice of low-flying aircraft and helicopters.

An investigation into the crash has already started and could take months, a Royal Navy spokesman said last night. The T4 sea training aircraft, one of four based at Yeovilton, was 30 minutes into the training flight when it crashed said Commander Vic Syrett, the base's Community Relations Officer. A qualified instructor was flying the two-man aircraft at the time. The Naval investigation is a bid to determine the cause of the accident.

Commander Syrett said the aircraft was not on a low level exercise when it crashed. He was not aware whether the two airmen had put out a May Day message or had tried to eject. The Yeovilton based Harriers fly up to 3,000 such training sorties each year, he said. The safety record of the aircraft type was good. The two-seater Harrier T-4 has been used to train Harrier pilots at Yeovilton since the early 1980s.

Upon reading this article I ran upstairs to the loft where a motley collection of cardboard boxes contains, amongst other things, the archives of the late lamented *Jon Downes and The Amphibians from Outer Space.*

A cursory look at the gig listings for the early part of 1996 confirmed my worst fears. We had indeed played two gigs at The *Merry Harriers* at Clayhidon. One in November 1995 and the other on the evening of Friday February 23rd 1996 - the same day that the ill fated Sea Harrier had crashed. This gig had been one of the final ones we had played during the last ill fated tour when both the band and my marriage were falling apart ignominiously around me and I was entering the state of semi catatonia which ended with my divorce and a massive nervous breakdown! No wonder I had forgotten the exact date of the incident.

Coming slowly down stairs I realised that with one major exception all the aspects of the case had been solved.

* We had already proved that `Badger` could not have been where he said he was at the time and place of the crash. This new evidence proved that everything he had told us about the crash was a complete pack of lies. The crash had taken place three months later than he had claimed, and furthermore it had happened in broad daylight so his story of witnessing shadowy shenanigans in the middle of a winter`s night was a complete tissue of lies.

* There was no RAF cover-up and indeed there never had been. When Wing Commander X told us that there were no records of an RAF crash in November 1995 he was telling us the absolute truth. Firstly the crash had not taken place until the February of the following year, and secondly, the aircraft in question had belonged to the Royal Naval Air Service rather than to the Royal Air Force. It was quite conceivable that the RAF Crash Inspectorate had no records of crashes involving RNAS aircraft, and even if they did, we had given them the wrong date and even the wrong year.

With British Armed Forces being geared up for a potentially costly and lengthy war in the Balkans, it was hardly surprising that an over worked RAF officer would devote only the minimum of time and effort in trying to unravel a mystery posed to him by a group of civilians from an obscure organisation that he had never heard of.

The only mystery left was why had first Danny, and then `Badger` spent so much time and energy in telling us the details of a mystery that was so easy to disprove? And, furthermore, why had they spent so much time and energy in telling exactly the same story to the three self-styled investigators of BUFOCRAPMORG in Bridgewater?

I was furiously angry. I don`t like people making a fool out of me, especially when this so-called "Mystery" turned out to be nothing of the kind, and had not only wasted a relatively substantial amount of time and energy, but was likely to cost me a fair amount of money as well.

It was time for me to bite back. I grabbed the telephone and rang the number that `Badger` had given us to contact him on. Much to my surprise he answered the `phone almost immediately.

"What the fucking hell do you think you are playing at you arsehole" I screamed down the telephone at him. *"Everything you`ve told us has been complete lies from start to finish! You`ve wasted my time, my money and my energy and if I ever see you again I`m going to break your fucking neck!!!"*

he muttered something shamefacedly about me having to talk to his brother, but I wasn`t listening..

"Fuck your brother and Fuck You!" I shouted, and slammed the `phone down. It was a pointless exercise in rage and personal abuse but at least it had the saving grace of making me feel a little better in the short term.

The various members of the CFZ posse then got on with their various routine activities, and I went to bed with a migraine brought on by rage and stress in equal measures.

Later that evening, Graham, Richard and I were sitting downstairs drinking wine and listening to *Led Zeppelin* when there was a knock at the door. I went to answer it and there to my great surprise were Basil and `Badger` looking surprisingly cheerful and surprisingly sane.

*"I think you`ve met my brother"* said Basil in a perfectly normal voice. `Badger` grinned at me slightly shamefacedly and said *"I think we owe you an explanation"*

163

"I think you do", I agreed, ushering them in and pouring them a glass of wine.

"It's simple really" explained Basil in a perfectly normal voice, without the slightest hint of hysteria or any mention of Bob Dylan lyrics. *"You guys were never meant to be involved.*

This all started as a practical joke on those idiots in Bridgewater. For years I've been going to the same pub as them and hearing their arrant bullshit, and I thought that it was about time that we turned the tables on them. BUFOCRAPMORG my arse! They are just a bunch of deluded idiots. One night `Badger` and I had been listening to them boring on about Roswell for about three hours and we decided to see quite how gullible they actually were, and so we spun them a ridiculous story about how that air crash at Wellington was actually caused by a mid air collision with a UFO.

They swallowed it hook line and sinker, and we continued to tell them more and more bizarre rubbish with the idea of testing them to see quite how much they would believe. `Badger was going to `submit` to some sort of phoney past life regression therapy and claim to have been abducted and we were even going to get a lamb carcass from the abattoir, mutilate the fucking thing, and drop it in the middle of the night on that stupid bitch Sandra`s front lawn just to see what happened......"

By this time we were all laughing hysterically.

Pouring myself another drink because by this stage I was convinced that I deserved it, I asked Basil why Danny had told us all about it......

"It's simple. he`s just a greedy little bastard. He`s been ripping me off for years, and a few months ago I finally threw him out. I'd had enough. He heard about this story from the loonies at BUFOCRAPMORG and must have believed it. I'm surprised that he was so gullible, but then again he swallowed all that hippy bullshit for years didn`t he?

He thought that here was his chance to make a few quid and decided to sell the story to you without telling me. When you contacted `Badger` I told him to keep the story up as well as he could, because by this stage

164

those bloody fools in Bridgewater were holding skywatches every week-end and trying to contact the `sky people` using morse-code and I didn`t want you bunch to spoil the joke!

I told `Badger` to try and come over like a drugged up drongo so you wouldn`t take him seriously. I hoped you guys would decide that his story was such crap that you wouldn`t bother to carry on".....

I looked at `Badger` in a new light.

"So he`s NOT a drugged up drongo" I asked

"No of course not......he works for the local Conservation council hence his nickname. It just sounds like the sort of stupid name that a drugged up hippy would have"...

Badger grinned at me......

"Yeah. I`d remembered a newspaper article about that escaped prisoner who hung out at the Fairmile camp and I just tossed it in to add a little verisimilitude..."

That settled it. Drugged up hippy drongos aren`t usually known for their use of words like `verisimilitude`. The whole explanation had the ring of truth about it.....

Clutching at straws I asked Basil why he had behaved so strangely the other night?

"I just thought that if I behaved like a complete prick then you`d proba-bly give up on the story. I didn`t want to have to admit that we`d made the whole thing up. When we first met, I`d been having psychiatric treat-ment and I decided to pretend to be a lunatic for the evening. A severe breakdown even on top of acid psychosis doesn`t necessarily make you into a raving lunatic for life y`know. You of all people should know that"...

He was right. I`d spent a large part of my last book The *Rising of the Moon* chronicling my own breakdown and subsequent diagnosis with manic depression. I`d then tried very hard to explain in writing how I was not a lunatic and how despite my illness I was still worthy of being taken seriously both as a writer and as a human being. Here I was hoist firmly by my own petard.

I had the good grace to look ashamed.

We chatted cheerfully to Basil and `Badger` for a while and then they went home and the party broke up.

The plot unfolds

Lying in bed that night with the dog I looked back upon the events of the previous few weeks. True, the Blackdown Mystery had turned out to have been a complete hoax, but as an Internet article on Somerset UFOs stated:

"Hoaxing is not a new phenomenon and in newspaper accounts published in Britain during April 1913 we learn how a number of Somerset folk became the victims of lights in the sky. These had appeared at night in the area over a period of two months, but the ruse was finally uncovered when shattered remnants of an enormous box-kite were finally recovered in the vicinity of the Mendip Hills. It appears the flying machine had been equipped with a large acetylene lamp and the hoaxers were eventually identified and caught after having been dumb enough to advertise for the lamp's return."

Because of the total gullibility of the worthies from BUFOCRAPMORG the story of the Blackdown Mystery had entered the canon of UFOlogical research. True, only an idiot would take these people seriously, but most independent researchers would not have bothered to go to Bridgewater and find out quite how inane these people actually were. In the absence of any evidence to the contrary the story was plausible enough. Let's face it, we had been at least partly fooled for several weeks, and we had been investigating the matter closely. If this story had got into the pages of *UFO Magazine* for example it would not have been long before it was accepted as fact. Eventually people would have written long, scholarly books about the incident, claiming that it was another British "Roswell", and yet another strand of disinformation would have been added to the already tangled web of contemporary UFOlogy.

In one way at least we had brought the affair to a satisfactory conclusion.

I didn't feel particularly good about my part in it, however. Desperate for evidence to support my own theory of causative fortean phenomena linked to quasi-independent Odyllic Life Energy I had allowed myself to be seduced into believing something because I wanted to believe it, and not because it made logical scientific sense.

Truly sometimes we believe what we want to believe, and see what we want to see, and allow ourselves to hypothesise complex explanations for things that don't really warrant them when, in the words of Sigmund Freud himself *"Sometimes a cigar is just a cigar"*

Smiling to myself, I turned over in bed, put my arms around the dog to cuddle him, and settled off to sleep.

EPILOGUE

Life at the CFZ continued as normal. I telephoned my publisher to tell him that we had solved the Blackdown Mystery and to tell him exactly what had happened and to offer to return my advance. Much to my surprise he laughed and told me to go ahead and write the book anyway. *"It`ll do the UFO Community good to see what a REAL investigation is like..warts and all"* he chuckled and to a certain extent I agreed with him.

Tony Healy stayed around the Westcountry for several weeks popping back to see us once in a while before disappearing off to Loch Ness for a while before he returned to Australia.

Graham reached a new personal best score on *Doom* and felt very pleased with himself for a few days. He also discovered a very noisy German heavy metal/dance band called *Rammstein* and he went around telling everyone who`d listen that they were the best thing he`d heard in years. Personally I thought that they were a bloody awful row but I couldn`t be bothered to argue [1].

Richard did his best to seduce a particularly irritating young woman that he`d met at the Goth night in a local pub. At the time of writing he had met with a singular lack of success but he still has high hopes of succeeding! Over the next month he continued writing his book on the natural history and mythology of Dragons [2], and drove the rest of us mad by playing *Sex Gang Children* loudly at every possible opportunity.

Basil went back to his solitary life in the middle of the Somerset Levels. A quiet, and slightly withdrawn man, he is content in his own company

---

1.   Seven years later, I - through the offices of my new girlfriend - have rescinded this opinion and now own several of their albums. *Rosenrot* (the latest waxing at time of press) is an absolutely wonderful record, and I am happy to recommend them to anyone who wants a listen.
2.   *Dragons: More than a Myth* was finally published by CFZ Press during the summer of 2005, and is a cracking good read

and although he could easily afford to live in an ordinary house and become part of what he calls "the suburban nightmare" he is quite happy
living in his little hut with his badger skins and his books, and we wish
him well.

I don`t know what happened to Danny. I`ve never heard from him again
although I have a sneaking suspicion that one day he will surface in my
life again as brash and as annoying as ever ready to lead me on yet another pointless wild goose chase.

In Bridgewater the three intrepid investigators of BUFOCRAPMORG
were deeply involved in another investigation after a girl that Sandra met
in the hairdressers claimed to have been abducted by Nazi Greys working for the covert world government.

In Walsall Nick Redfern bought four more *Ramones* bootlegs as a present to himself after the successful launch of his third best seller, and the
manager of a band called *Prolapse* continued to negotiate with Britain`s
Fox Mulder for him to make at least one vocal contribution to their next
compact disc..

In London, PM Tony Blair looked out of his study window at the small
gaggle of peace protesters outside and mused on his new found knowledge that it IS possible to fool most of the people most of the time, while
outside the entrance to Downing Street, the team of Police Officers still
operated their ad hoc vehicle check point, and in a bunker forty stories
below Whitehall, a captured alien grey demanded another helping of
strawberry ice cream and started to laugh...........

"Well the moral of this story -- the moral of this song,
is that one should never be where one should not belong,
and if you see a traveller, help him with his load,
and don`t go mistaking paradise for that home across the road"

Bob Dylan *The Ballad of Frankie Lee and Judas Priest* 1968

FINISMO

Nota Bene

To bring the story up to date:

- Toby, the CFZ Dog died of cancer at the age of 15 on June 1st 2000

- Nick Redfern spoke at the 2001 International UFO Congress in Nevada where he met a charming young lady called Dana. Six months later they were married and living in Texas

- Jester no longer has anything to do with the CFZ

- Graham, Richard and I (together with artist Mark North and new boy John Fuller) continue to fight a rearguard action to save forteana from the clutches of those who believe too much

THE CFZ IN THE BAD OLD DAYS

(Pix Nick Redfern

About the author............

Jonathan Downes was born in Portsmouth in 1959, and spent much of his childhood in Hong Kong where, surrounded by age-old Chinese superstitions and a dazzlingly diverse range of exotic wildlife, he soon became infected with the twin passions for exotic zoology and the paranormal which were to define his adult life. He spent some years as a nurse for the mentally handicapped but began writing professionally in the late 1980s. He has now written over twenty books. He is also a musician and songwriter who has made a number of critically acclaimed but commercially unsuccessful albums.

In 1992 he founded The Centre for Fortean Zoology, with the aim of coordinating research into mystery animals, bizarre and aberrant animal behaviour and his own particular love of zooform phenomena (paranormal entities which only appear to be animals!)

He has searched for Lake Monsters at Loch Ness, pursued sea serpents and the grotesque Cornish owlman—which inspired his most famous book *The Owlman and Others* - chased big cats across westcountry moorland, and in 1998 and 2004 went to Latin America in search of the grotesque vampiric Chupacabra. He is a popular public speaker both in the UK and the United States, where he regularly appears at conventions talking about his many expeditions and his latest research projects.

He is also an activist for Mental Health issues, having suffered with Bipolar Disorder (Manic Depression) for many years. In 2005, after having lived in Exeter for 20 years, he moved to his old family home in Woolsery, North Devon, where he intends to establish a full-time Visitor's Centre and museum for the Centre for Fortean Zoology. Following his father's death in February 2006, he inherited the old family home and announced that construction of the museum and research facility later in the year.

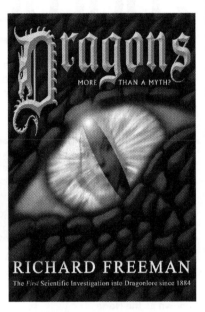

Other books available from
CFZ PRESS

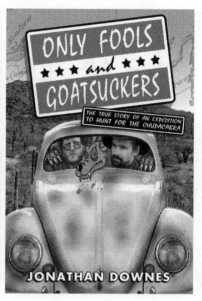

Other books available from
CFZ PRESS

CFZ PRESS

THE BEAST AND I

In this extraordinarily funny book about the "Beast of Bodmin". Paul Crowther tells us of the adventures of "The Beast and I" and, along the way, introduces us to such engaging characters as the female vicar who risked life and limb to observe a beast at close quarters, the zoo-keeper with a portfolio of pictures of a domestic moggie, `Mr Angry` (who was annoyed to find a picture of his pet cat plastered all over the local newspaper, captioned - as "The Beast"), and - of course - `Lara` the lynx of old London town.

ISBN 0-9512872-4-9

WHILE THE CAT'S AWAY

Over the past thirty years or so there have been numerous sightings of large exotic cats, including black leopards, pumas and lynx, in the South West of England. Former Rhodesian soldier Sam McCall moved to North Devon and became a farmer and pub owner when Rhodesia became Zimbabwe in 1980. Over the years despite many of his pub regulars having seen the "Beast of Exmoor" Sam wasn't at all sure that it existed. Then a series of happenings made him change his mind.

Chris Moiser—a zoologist—is well known for his research into the mystery cats of the westcountry. This is his first novel.

ISBN: 0-9512872-1-4

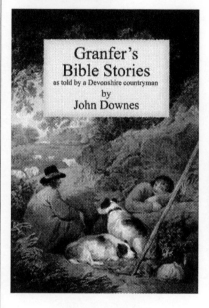
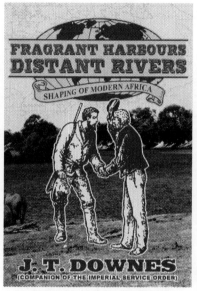